PASSION FORMULA

THE NEW CUSTOMER EXPERIENCE

Marty D. Fish, CFE

In memory of Lisa

Every individual customer experience matters. It is not a matter of quantity, but of the quality of our service that will determine our success.

Contents

How to Use This Book

Written in an entertaining, futuristic, space-age setting, this book contains useful Elements and Pixels that will guide you on your journey to customer service excellence. *Elements* are important notes extracted from each chapter, which have been broken into their most fundamental components. Elements should be observed carefully, as they are designed to be applied practically in order to properly generate the Passion Formula.

Pixels are real, but semi-fictionalized, case studies, which have very specific points. Just like the points, or pixels, on a computer screen, they join together to create a complete picture. It is advised that the reader study each Pixel and extract the primary points from them, concisely making notes to discern what the primary points are. If a case study has a detrimental outcome, the reader should consider how it could have been handled differently in order to achieve the optimal customer experience. If the outcome is positive, the reader should also consider what fundamental aspects were in play in order to achieve the desired effect. For further consideration, Pixels are examined deeper in the back of this book as a Feature item, "Pixel Exploration." It is vital that the reader study each exploratory, preferably after reading the related Pixel in order to gain a deeper understanding of the point being made in each Pixel case study.

Features are the attachments listed in the back of the book. In the same fashion that accessories on a fully decked-out new car serve as bonus features, these addendums are bonuses that may be used to help the reader achieve phenomenal customer experiences.

It is important to understand that in order to fully understand this book, the reader must not simply read the stories, elements, pixels, and features merely for entertainment purposes. The reader is encouraged to focus on the fundamental underlying philosophy that pervades throughout. The philosophy is key. Developing an atmosphere of superb customer experiences comes from having a mindset that fully grasps this philosophy. Once it is grasped, it is easy to digest, believe, and implement. The implementation of the philosophy will then breathe new life and hope into you and your company; it will give a renewed sense of purpose to all who envelop themselves within it.

Preface

Sodium. Chemical symbol: Na. It is a soft, silver, highly reactive metal. Formulate it with chlorine and you have common table salt. Combine sodium with water, however, and you have an intense explosion of power and energy.

The words you are reading right now are a powerful chemical composition for incendiary customer service success. As you read this formula, my hope is that you experience an intense feeling of transformation from salt into silvery, gleaming sodium. May this book wash down all over your mind and body like water pouring upon shimmering sodium, igniting passion for success, so that you become a beautiful, reactive glistening element, with power and grandeur – explosive, glorious – this is what it means to possess the passion formula!

Allow your eyes to permeate deeper within these pages with great hunger and expectation, and you may receive what you desire. This is the new customer experience that can transform you, your workplace, your customers, and your business as you know it. I encourage you to embrace it, and enjoy it passionately.

This is the business alchemy of transmutation from lead into gold - the new business formula – let it transform how you live.

Enjoy, with pleasure!

PASSION FORMULA

Chapter 1

Embrace Her

Imagine … you and I are clutching hands, ready to embark on a journey through the cosmos together. I turn to look you in the eyes before we launch, and with great apprehension I say, "I have something … important to tell you." You can feel the anxiety welling up inside of you; you turn toward me and reply, "Tell me. What is it?"

"Though we will be travelling light years to fulfill our mission, we will have another passenger who must travel with us… we have no choice. There is no other way." You respond. "Oh no, who is it?" I hesitate, but then answer, "It is … your employer!" The entity enters the pod.

Tears. Screams. Cries of pain. The fumes of torment and agony fill the small vessel. The walls of the capsule rattle. After the bitter shrieks die and decay into the far reaches of space, falling on your knees, you mutter, "Why? Why? Why?"

With heartfelt empathy and care, I look down at you and say, "There is no other way. Without the employer, we cannot survive the journey. It is of crucial importance that it go with us. Only it has the resources and knowledge to save our lives from the harshness of deep space. Stand up. I want you to come here and let me show you something."

You arise; I slowly lead you to the daunting thing. You pause and cry out, "No, I can't! It's too hideous!" I reply, "There, now, don't be afraid. It's okay. It won't hurt you." The being stands glowering over us, intimidating. You can feel the hair stand on end as shivers sparkle and dance across your spine. I reach up to touch a small thread dangling from the chest of the beast. As you look closer, you see that the being is covered with dark forms and documents, which make it look overpowering. You spy a document with the words, "Articles of Incorporation." Another says, "Form I-9;" you then see other documents, "W4," "W2," "Stock Certificates," etc. You whisper, "Oh my! What is this?"

I pull the string. The creature begins to unravel, forms peeling off of it. You scream as documents scatter and litter the craft. Like a butterfly, the entity sheds its old skin, revealing a glorious, beautiful sight to behold. Light bursts forth; glimmering radiance fills the capsule. The beautiful form of a shimmering woman is revealed. She looks like a goddess. "What is it?" you ask.

With a smile, I respond, "This is your employer. This is her true form and nature." You can't believe it and say, "How is this possible? Why did I not see this before? I … I … I never knew!"

I continue, "You see, you have been looking at her in the wrong way. She is not some beast that exists to torture you and chain you to the desk of hell for eternity. She does not desire to steal your dreams and suck your life from you until you are old, feeble, and ebbing away. You were looking at her with the wrong eyes and heart. Under the exterior of her legal forms, policies, and regulations, she is quite lovely. She truly does care for you and wants to help you live life to the fullest. She already provides for you; she takes care of you when you are sick. She has always been there for you. Believe it or not, she truly loves you. I know you cannot fathom that, but she does.

PIXEL 1 – *Space-Fly*

A sign vendor was working diligently, outside his client's store. He was installing window lettering just around the corner from the store's front door. The store, called "Space-Fly," sold rocket-boards, which are like flying skateboards, but the owner was hardly ever there. Her business was in a professional office complex where she paid a hefty monthly rent, but she preferred to stay home most of the time, and her store was only open two days a week, for four hours per day. She did have a sign in the window that stated, "Call for an appointment," and it listed her cellphone just underneath. She wanted the massive signs installed, in order to drum up more business, because her profits were suffering greatly. The sign vendor was there for most of the day, installing the large vinyl signs. As he did, he noticed many potential customers come to the front door, attempting to open it. When they realized it was locked, they walked away. One gentleman came to the store that morning to find it closed, but he returned again that afternoon. He tried hard to pull the door open and he started looking through the tinted windows to see if anyone was inside. The sign vendor, noticing the man's

---

PIXEL 1 – *Space-Fly (Continued)*

frustration, walked around the corner and said, "Sir, do you need some help?" The man replied, "Yeah! I've come here for the last few days and no one is ever here!" Are they out of business?" The sign vendor said, "Oh, no, the owner only works by appointment," and he pointed to the sign in the window. "You could give her a call." The man grew more frustrated; he turned around and left.

What should the store owner do to create a quality experience for her customers, which would also help her achieve her goal of increasing profitability?

"From this moment on, you are to both become best friends … even lovers. I want you to fall in love with her. She doesn't want you to give her eight hours a day; she doesn't want your full-time commitment. She wants your full-life commitment. If you will take her hand, right now, and accept her as your very own true love, she will do even greater things for you. She will show you great pleasures, joys, and success. She has the power to give you everything you truly dream of and desire, but you must first plunge deeply in love with her; become one with her. Embrace her. This is the only way we can safely reach our destination.

"Our journey together is a long one and I think you will find that now that you can see her true nature, it is going to be an amazing adventure. Now, let's get buckled up together with our newfound love and finish what we set out to do. I'm about to hit hyper-drive so that we will be thrust into the deep recesses of business space."

Element 1 (E1): *Embrace your employer. Love her deeply.*

PASSION FORMULA

Chapter 2

Pendulum

Enter the mechanical, corporate world, "Pendulum." Known as the "Great Silver Giant," it is a sphere existing in an otherworldly dimension of time and space. Inside this cold orb slowly and gently sways a colossal, glowing pendulum. This is the planet of the entities. A prime entity, called "Zee Eoh," rules above all the other sentient beings in this realm. Zee is the keeper of the pendulum.

Every three years, Zee reverses the pendulum and propels it into another direction. This causes a massive flurry of action and energy among the entities. Each new phase of the pendulum launches a new mechanical system that tells the entities what to do.

After releasing the pendulum, Zee stands atop the orb. With a deep, booming voice, he boldly announces, "I am Zee Eoh, the great and powerful. There is none other in the whole universe like unto me. I am the sovereign of this great world among worlds. Heed my voice! My loyal subjects, I announce something new to you today. I, and I alone, have chosen to change the direction of the great pendulum. Yes, with this new swing, our world will transform into a magnificent utopia of light. This is the new way. I assure you that you will follow this new swing of the pendulum and everything you desire will come true. We will become the greatest planet in the galaxy!"

The entities erupt into praise and worship of their great leader, shouting, "All hail the great Zee Eoh! Master of all!" The entities, as they always did every few years,

21

begin to implement the new ways of the pendulum. They work hard and do all they can to see that they achieve every goal that Zee sets for them through the new shift.

After the pendulum arcs past its midpoint, its swing grows slower; so do the efforts of the entities. Grumbling is heard among a few of them and chaos ensues. The great changes, once promised to the entities and their planet, do not occur. In truth, nothing changes; it never does. This enrages some of the entities and they form new assemblies to express their wrath. Some of the assemblies rebel against the pendulum, crying, "Destroy the pendulum!" Others shout, "Purge Zee Eoh! Remove him from among us! He did this to us, and he must now perish!" Others rally behind them, until the whole world is enflamed with turmoil. This causes the Great Silver Giant to become a world of war, barren and desolate.

As had happened every few years, the ruler was condemned and cast into the Exhortian pit of death, while another with the same name was put in his place. The new Zee Eoh stands atop the orb and, like his predecessors, announces the new swing of the pendulum. The new phase begins.

This is the life cycle for the corporate world, Pendulum. It was vibrant in its origin, but as the pendulum swings through the decades, due to its never-ending system shifts, it is doomed to lose its momentum and die. What the entities fail to recognize is that the solution to their world's woes does not lie in the pendulum or in the systems that it generates. The answer lies elsewhere.

Systems are nothing more than machines. Machines are non-caring, non-feeling. They are incapable of saving their planet, because machines are not living. The entities misplace their trust in the machines and eventually they are led astray and suffer because of it, even to the point of their death.

If they do not make a massive paradigm change, their world will implode and be destroyed. They must evolve their world and reformulate their existence.

WARNING – HIGHLY CORROSIVE ELEMENT

Element 2 (E2): *Corporate change. It is injected into a corporate body, usually by a new executive leader. This element is unstable in nature. It may be accepted by the corporate body at first, but after the reaction occurs, it may slowly undergo a process of violent rejection. If not controlled by other stable elements (such as element Be1, etc.), its powerful oxidization nature will cause the executive(s) to be eliminated, quite possibly destroying the whole of the corporate body.*

PIXEL 2 –*Call of the Alien Worms*

A small boy came home from school one day and he threw his hover-pack on the floor, like he did every day. Later that night, his mother came into his room to pull his lunchbox out of the pack. As she did, she saw something wiggling out of the corner of her eye; it was an alien worm. She screamed at the top of her lungs. Alien worms are the worst kind of parasites a home could have, and her son had just brought some home with him. Alien worms reproduce asexually at enormous rates and they can bore through any solid material with their laser tentacles, completely demolishing an establishment in only a matter of days. She shot at it with her pocket phaser and blew it into pieces, but it was too late, she noticed several other worms already burning holes through her floor. She ran into her living room with a hunk of the charred worm and threw it at the feet of her husband, screaming, "Look what your son brought home!"

The husband glanced down at it and blurted out, "What the heck! Alien worms? What do you want me to do about it?" She screeched, "Do something!" He replied, "Why don't you call one of those exterminator services." She shook her head at him, frustrated, and went to her computer. She quickly searched for, "alien worm exterminators." A whole list of service providers popped up on her screen.

PIXEL 2 –*Call of the Alien Worms (Continued)*

She called the first one that popped up.

"Thank you for calling AAA-Worm Exterminators. We are not available to take your call. Please leave your name, number, and the reason for your call, and we will get back to you within 24 hours." She hung up, not leaving a message, and muttered to herself, "24 hours? My house will be a pile of rubbish in 24 hours." She called the next number listed.

She heard a strong alien accent answer her call. "Groc, borg. Hoo mey ooh zep hoo?" She stammered, being thrown off by the strange dialect, and responded, "...um, is this GB Exterminators?" The voice replied, "Zee, Groc Borg." She was frustrated and hung up, muttering again, "You've got to be kidding me." She called several more services, and was answered by robots, machines, or unintelligible alien receptionists, making her more frustrated with each experience, until she reached AWE-xterminators.

"Thank you for calling AWE-xterminators. This is Axia. How may I assist you?" She thought, 'finally, a real person,' "Yes, I have an emergency. My son brought home some alien worms from school and they are destroying my house. Can you help?" Axia responded, "Absolutely! If you give me your name, address, and phone number, I'll be there

PIXEL 2 –*Call of the Alien Worms (Continued)*

myself within 30-minutes." She couldn't believe it and said, "You are a lifesaver!" She gave him her information and he concluded the call, "Mrs. Miller, you can set your mind at ease. I assure you that I will destroy every last one of those worms, before you go to bed tonight. This is what we do, and we do it best! I'll see you within half an hour." He hung up; she felt great relief.

As promised, Axia arrived within 30 minutes and he destroyed all the alien worms within one hour. She was so happy that she referred AWE-xterminators to all her friends via social networks. AWE-xterminators, within a short period of time, became the leading extermination service within the entire metropolitan area.

Which service-provider won Mrs. Miller's business, making her a loyal customer? Why? What policies do you think this business set in place to guarantee quality customer experiences?

Chapter 3

Xiggy

One month before …

Xiggy is my personal robot. He is a fully automated Xt3250 Generation android. My associate in the cubicle next to me is jealous, because he still has the old Px2349 version (sucks to be him). Anyway, I got Xiggy as a gift from my boss, along with a generous holiday bonus (I love my boss!)

Xiggy is what is called a "Genibot." Unlike the "smart" droids from years ago, Xiggy is a genius robot. He knows everything there is to know about anything and everything. In short, he's sort of a smart aleck, but you've got to love him – he's an SP, meaning Systems Processor - he can get the work done. We have a little term for SP's that we use when they can't hear us. It's "Sprocs," but don't tell HR. They consider it derogatory, and it ticks some droids off. Xiggy is alright, though. He doesn't seem to care.

The bad thing about Xiggy is that he has no heart – literally. He does not care one iota about me, our customers, our work, our mission, or our vision. He is a great system-processor though, but that is all he was programmed to do.

My company's name is Xamron, Inc. We produce the world's finest Neuro-Enhancers; they're basically brain chips. Parents bring their kids into our stores and we inject the nano-chips right into their pre-frontal cortexes.

It's relatively painless, but it increases their IQ to well over 200. In short, we produce little Savants and Einsteins.

Recently, the Vice President of our Training Team issued an announcement that we are to implement a new system called CSP. That stands for "Customer Support Program." It's not really a new program, as we had tried it several years ago without much success. But, that's what our company does. Every few years it announces a new program, and being faithful, hard-working employees, we implement it along with our Sprocs.

Though Xiggy is the latest model, his charging system is still a bit antiquated in my opinion. He uses batteries, but that's okay. Don't get me wrong, the company that produced Xiggy uses the best long-life organic batteries, fully rechargeable, harnessing energy using the electrochemistry of organic molecules rather than metals, like lithium. Nevertheless, he only holds a charge for about, say, maybe eight hours. Then he's useless, a lot like some of my colleagues … me included. I roll him into the closet to recharge there until the next morning.

"Notice, to all associates," a voice announced through our Sprocs, "The CSP is to be implemented and programmed into all personal robots immediately. The new program data is being streamed into them directly, now. Commence program initiation immediately."

After Xiggy received the full program, he buzzed, "Installing… initializing… download complete. Activating program." Xiggy did have a humanoid voice, but it had a buzzing twinge to it. It could get annoying sometimes. I enquired, "Xiggy, tell me about this new program. Is there anything new?" He droned back, "As an associate of Xamron, over time you have seen various strategies and focus areas that we have used as a company to improve our customers' experience at stores and to work effectively with their store managers. And as you know, we plan to prioritize rebuilding our relationship with customers in a number of ways. One is by re-considering some of our policies. Another is by confirming the fundamental way we interact and work with customers by bringing back the Customer Support Program as the basis for working together."

Xiggy's chest, a luminous screen, lit up to reveal a chart. He continued, "Here is the current version of the Customer Support Program. We have made some very small changes from the year 2098 version, but I think you will find it quite familiar. We plan to discuss it at trainings through the year."

The chart summed up the program in just five steps. I guess it seemed positive and inspiring enough. Maybe it would work better than before. Every phase had a paragraph to explain it, but yep, it was the exact same program. Oh well. If that's what upper management wanted, I guess we had no choice. "Get at it Xiggy," I said, and he whirred off to implement the new program.

The months passed. The program worked just like before; the machine cranked out the standard results as upper management had expected. I could hear Xiggy in the distance speaking on his cellular unit. He performed his script in the same droning fashion, "Hello. Thank you for calling Xamron. Would you be interested in our free cognitive testing special?" It was a new customer. He answered the questions and, as usual, he scheduled the customer to visit one of our stores to have her child tested.

To implement the CSP, our company typically had weekly team meetings. In reality, associates sat in conference rooms with stark manager-bots, who told about new updates and policies. Manager-bots aren't friendly or sociable, but they are competent. All they are programmed to do is manage and give orders. After our first CSP introductory meeting, Xiggy announced new memos from headquarters about the CSP and he gave us a new goal. What we had was never really a team collaboration. Sitting in corporate meetings was tantamount to being tortured – it felt like my life was being sucked out of my skull by ravenous alien leeches. I would rather listen to a thousand metal-clawed androids scratch their tinny fingernails on a thousand chalkboards, than sit in on those meetings. They were grueling for all us who were human.

PIXEL 3 – *Fizzy Parties*

Vebo was planning to have a fizzy party to celebrate his daughter's sixth birthday. Fizzy parties are extremely popular among children. In order to conduct a fizzy party, one must have a zero-gravity unit, which looks a bit like an enclosed trampoline. The unit is surrounded by a clear plastic wall. The base of the unit is large and round; it encases the zero-gravity unit. People like to pour water into the top of the unit, which makes the water break apart and float,

PIXEL 3 – *Fizzy Parties (Continued)*

resembling bubbles in a glass of soda water; hence the name fizzy party. Children enter the fizzy chamber and float around; they catch the water balls and hurl them at each other, like they might do with water balloons. It's a lot of fun.

Vebo was shopping around at various fizzy stores looking for accessories to make the party fun. At one store, he found a Z-G Party Box, which is a cooler that keeps beverages on ice. It attaches to the outside of the zero-gravity unit. It was neat-looking and would have been the perfect addition to his party. Unfortunately it said, "Assembly Required," on the box. "Dang," he thought. He asked the clerk, "Do you have any of these that are already assembled?" The clerk replied, "No, and they are not easy to assemble. I bought one; it was a pain." Vebo had the money, and price was not an issue, but he did not have the time to put the cooler together; nor did he want to. Vebo hated putting anything together that required assembly. He would almost always lose a screw, bolt, or some piece, and he usually seemed to have an extra mystery piece left over. "The guy who invented 'Assembly Required' should be shot," he said to himself.

Several days later, Vebo entered a different store, which had a whole line of Z-G Party Boxes displayed at the front. He looked at them admiringly and turned to the clerk, "I'd sure love to have one of

PIXEL 3 – *Fizzy Parties (Continued)*

these. You wouldn't be able to sell me a pre-assembled one, would you?" The clerk responded, "Sure, that's how we sell them. They are all assembled." Vebo said, "No way! I was in another store and they said assembly was required. The clerk said, with a grin, "That's what makes us the number one store! Our managers assemble these in their spare time, so they're used to it, and it's easy for them." With excitement, Vebo said, "Great! I'll take one!" He left, a happy and satisfied customer.

Which business ultimately profited from the product labeled, "Assembly Required"? Which business went the extra mile for its customers? What do you think led the second business to start assembling its Z-G Party Boxes for its customers for free?

I had been working for Xamron for about 15 years. As time passed, I realized that I was becoming Xiggy, seriously. I felt like a cold, heartless robot, cranking out work in a lifeless manner. I came in at 8:30 am, and clocked out every day at 5:00 pm sharp. I gave what was expected, at the bare minimum, and no more, just like Xiggy. But, unlike Xiggy, I looked forward to Friday, and dreaded Sunday, because it meant I would have to return to work within 24 hours.

Normally, my job is to work with store managers. One day, I was on the phone talking to a manager, regurgitating my script as I always did. I gazed at my computer screen, typing notes into my database to document our conversation. I was empty and lifeless. I hung up the phone. At that exact moment, my phone and Xiggy's both rang. We both answered and spoke exactly at the same rhythm, in the same tone, with the same words, "Thank you for calling Xamron. How may I assist you?" I looked over at Xiggy and he looked at me, recognizing the same thing that I did. It was like looking into a mirror. I had become Xiggy. I was a robot.

This is life at Xamron. It's not much, but it's a job. It has its good side and its bad side. What it really comes down to is this: It's a paycheck; it pays the bills.

PASSION FORMULA

Chapter 4

The Outbreak

The following day at lunch, I happened to be sitting in the break room eating the same meager rations that I had eaten in that same spot, day after day, for years: Gazorkian curried soup. It wasn't much, but it was sustenance. I glanced down at the electronic news-pad on the table and I spied an article that caught my attention. I was startled. It read:

NEWS REPORT – Robotitus Outbreak

Do you have a loved one who stares at a computer-screen doing his work for hours without emotion? Does he perform work like an android, without excitement or passion? Does he go through the motions daily, working like a robot? Does he act bored and uninterested in doing anything? Chances are, your loved one has … *Robotitus*.

"I never thought it could happen to Harold," says a local woman about her husband, who recently succumbed to the new and unusual disease. "He used to be such a cheerful, fun-loving sort of fellow. But look at him now. All he does is sit at his computer doing his work like a robot, clickity-click, tappity-tap; he just punches buttons with no expression at all. Hey, Harold! Do you wanna sandwich? I'll make your favorite … pastrami on rye." She paused for a response, "See … nothing! He's a robot, I tell ya'! I even gave him a teaspoon of Robo-tussin, but nothing seems to work! I'm at my wit's end, I tell ya'!"

Recent accounts of this new pandemic appear to be sweeping the nation. Employees everywhere are showing similar symptoms: blank expressions, drone-like personalities, monotone responses, poor customer service."

Oh my, I thought, I've got Robotitus! How could this happen to me? I could not believe it, yet I knew I couldn't tell anyone. They would label me as a mental patient, or freak, but I reflected all the symptoms. I read on …

"So, how does one become cured of this dreaded disease? Dr. Obe Zimbawe, chief neurologist from the CogniBot Psychological Institute, shared with us the following. "This is a growing epidemic, but it is not just an employee sickness; it's symptomatic of unhealthy companies, who are culpable for this illness as well. Corporations just aren't innovative anymore! They aren't inspiring and impacting their employees nowadays like they used to." When asked how employees could be saved from this horrible disease, Dr. Zimbawe said, "Get them away from work and computers for at least a week. You must isolate the victims from mundane work and anything electronic; make them think independently, on their own. I know that is difficult to do, but the victims must break away from their job so they will once again realize that they are indeed human. Now, after the isolation period, the best way to cure them from this malady is to shock them out of it. I don't mean with electroshock therapy, though that may work, but you must put them in an intensely exciting professional development activity or program, in which they may be inspired to accomplish something purposeful in life; that's important. It must *create purpose* for them. Next, have them work with a mentor who inspires them. This is the key! If the afflicted person discovers inspiration through a deeply inspiring mentor, he is capable of not only being cured of his illness, he may accomplish something great, for the good of all mankind. Finally, employees need to be innovative; they must be able to contribute and exert their creativity. That is what separates humans from robots. This is the regimen I would prescribe. Otherwise, if employees don't follow these steps, they, and their employers, could suffer from roboticide, which is tantamount to corporate death!"

That's it! That's what I needed to do. I needed to get away from work. I didn't want to be doomed to a life as a human robot, so I decided to take the doctor's advice. I would take some personal leave. I needed it badly, anyway. Our company had great benefits and my manager was always the best about giving me time off when I asked for it, so I did. I would quietly sneak off and cure myself. I had no desire to be a victim of roboticide.

Element 3 (E3): Reprogram your mind. Withdraw. Refocus. Your purpose must be to change your daily pattern, or routine, and realign your mental status quo to become healthier. This may mean that you need to spend a week with an inspirational guru you admire, or that you should attend a motivational boot camp or inspirational event. Regardless, you must determine that whatever activity you choose to undertake, it must reboot your cognitive faculty well enough that you do not return with the same mental state as when you left. This must be accomplished on a regular basis.

Element 4 (E4): *Cling to a passionate mentor. Your mentor does not necessarily need to be someone in your field of work or study. He or she does, however, have to be someone inspirational, who will cause you to catch the fires of passion so that you can continue to burn with motivation and fervency after you depart.*

Element 5 (E5): *Create. Allow yourself to be innovative and creative in your role. Approach your supervisor and suggest new ideas that will increase productivity or will inspire your associates. Innovation will fuel your passion and will generate more excitement about what you do.*

PIXEL 4 – *Creepy Chicken*

LightSpeed is the largest fast-food restaurant chain in the galaxy. It has fairly good food at reasonable prices. They have strong name brand recognition and are practically everywhere. LightSpeed has a solid customer base because their standards are high when it comes to food quality and marketing. They strive to hire good employees, but they are sometimes weak in this area. Since they are open for business 24 hours a day, seven days a week, they have difficulty finding quality employees who want to work the graveyard shift. So, they often take what they can get. They frequently hire unprofessional extra-terrestrials from other planets, because such employees are desperate to work, or their sleeping habits are different from ours, so they don't mind working at night. The challenge is that these aliens don't speak human languages well, so they have poor communication skills.

One particular time, a customer named Flux was travelling with some companions at approximately 2:30 am. He hovered his craft up to the fly-through menu. Over the intercom system, he heard an alien voice, "Weeekom zu Lee-spee. Arder weeen rye-deee." Flux looked at his friends and they snickered. One of them whispered, "It's a Gazorkian. You'd think they would hire someone who could actually speak our language." Flux whispered back, "Shhh,

PIXEL 4 – *Creepy Chicken (Continued)*

he'll hear you." He was concerned because he knew Gazorkians had quick tempers, and he didn't want to take a chance with this one slathering a slimy tentacle on his food.

He turned back to the intercom and said, "Yes, I'm ready. I would like a chicken sandwich combo and a large Cosmic-Cola, please." The intercom answered back, "Weeed ju leek creepy ooh krid?" Flux paused, confused; he looked at his friends and whispered, "What did he say?" One started laughing out loud. Flux turned back to the intercom and stammered, "I … I'm sorry, what was that?" The Gazorkian must have heard the laughing and prattled back, angrily, "Zu leek zeee creepy chiggin ooh krid?" The friend burst out laughing, "I think he said, 'Do you want the creepy chicken! Bwah, ha, ha, ha…" Flux said, "Shut up, man," but by that time, all his friends were laughing. Even Flux became tickled and couldn't help snickering. The Gazorkian was growing impatient, "Ahh zeeed 'CREEPY' ooh 'KRID!'" This made even Flux erupt with laughter. The whole craft was bouncing with hilarity and the Gazorkian started yelling at them in what they guessed was his own alien tongue, "Flaark zu, zeee flarken boozdids!..." They had no idea what he said, but Flux said, "We better get out of here. There is no way I'm eating here now. Who knows what he

PIXEL 4 – *Creepy Chicken (Continued)*

would do to my sandwich." His friend laughed, "Hey, maybe that's why they call it the 'creepy chicken!'" They laughed uncontrollably and sped off to find another fast-food restaurant.

Why do you think the employer placed someone in the position to work with customers if the employee has poor communication and customer skills? In the transaction, ultimately, did the employer win or lose? How many other customers do you think LightSpeed loses on a regular basis? How do you think this impacts LightSpeed's brand image and profitability?

PASSION FORMULA

Chapter 5

Farin

I decided to take one week of personal leave and visit the planet Abacabar with my oldest daughter. Abacabar was known as the party planet. It seemed like a great place to take a break from work and computers. My daughter wanted to go, because she was 19 years old and she wanted to get a certification while there to make, what they call, "Brain-Fuzzy" drinks. They had a top academy on the planet and she planned to get her certification. Her goal was to become certified and take a one-year contract on the planet Qaart as a brain-fuzzy drink bartender. By doing that, she could make enough money to pay for her college.

Abacabar was a phenomenal planet. It was red and black; not pretty, but it was fantastically surrealistic. Music could be heard everywhere; anywhere you looked, there were brain-fuzzy drinks. I took my daughter to her academy, trying to avoid the strange aliens and brain-fuzzy vendors; when we arrived, I met a being who changed my life. Her name was Farin.

Farin was an Instructor at the academy and she was a blue space pixie. Farin was full of energy, and flitted from place to place. Upon entering the academy, Farin flitted up to us and announced, "Welcome to the academy! I am so excited that you could be here." My daughter said to me, "Dad, this is Farin! She's the one I told you about." My daughter was impressed with Farin. She told me that Farin actually managed the academy. She said that Farin personally answered the phone when she called and that she was so friendly to her that it made her want to sign up, without even seeing the academy. She explained that she had called several other academies, but droids answered their phones, and they weren't nice to her at all. They didn't care if she enrolled or not. But, when she called Farin, she gave out her personal cellphone number and told her to call at any time, day or night.

Farin was excitable and passionate about her work. She led us into her classroom and with great fervor told us all about the courses and how she was there to help us. She asked us questions about ourselves and took a deep interest in us. She was an amazing creature. In fact, because she did such a great job, I decided to enroll in the one-week course too, along with my daughter. I didn't have any reason to learn how to make brain-fuzzy drinks, but I was curious to learn more from Farin. I would become her student. Maybe, I thought, I could be cured of my Robotitus.

We started classes. Farin taught with great enthusiasm. I took notes and wrote down all she said. She told stories about her former students and her experiences in life. She told how she met her pixie spouse at that very academy, ten years ago. He was once a student of hers. We learned how to make fuzzy-cocktails and drinks I never knew existed. It was obvious that she cared for her students. If anyone was not able to come to class, she would immediately call them and make other arrangements to ensure they didn't miss anything. Sometimes, her customers would call at 3:00 in the morning and she was there for them. She always had a smile on her face and was always engaging.

The week flew by like a whirlwind and we had to get back on the spaceship to return home. I was sad we had to go. Before we left, Farin said to us all, "My students, I have loved every minute of my time with each and every one of you. You are now a part of my family. I want you to know that I am always here for you. Anytime you want to come back for more classes, you are welcome here, and it will be at no charge. If you ever need help, call me at any time – I'm serious. I want to thank you for sharing your lives with me. I wish you well on your journeys home." Then, with a smile, she flicked her pixie dust and disappeared before our very eyes.

Element 6 (E6): Personal ownership. Empowerment. Whether the employee has tangible shares in the company or not, he/she must be granted personal ownership of it. The employer must instill the sense of personal ownership within every associate. This element generates allegiance, and strong feelings of commitment toward the employer. Every associate must become a devotee. This empowerment is the catalyst to creating great customer service.

Element 7 (E7): Customer engagement. Inspire and engage the customer. Use this "element of surprise" by giving them service beyond their expectations. Consider what the customer would expect from the typical transaction and give them more to the point where they say, "Wow!" That is the proper amount of this element that must be added to the successful customer experience equation.

Element 8 (E8): *Model the experience. The employer must model the sensation of corporate passion to its employees with intensity. It is the employer's responsibility to inspire, excite, and motivate associates. Employees must strive to stir up the power of passion within themselves. They, too, must exemplify this experience to their customers.*

Element 9 (E9): *Court your customer. Make him/her a part of your family. Instill personal feelings of trust, so that your customer grows 100% loyal to you. Court each new customer, as you would court a new potential spouse. Give them your full commitment and expect theirs in return. Engage them and experience a wonderful business marriage, for life.*

PIXEL 5 – *Smellians*

After humans discovered how to travel beyond light speed, it opened our universe up to all kinds of visiting sentient creatures. One class of aliens was from the planet Smetna. These aliens had a strong odor to them, and that is why they have unfortunately been called, "Smellians." It's not that they are bad or dirty at all; it's just that they have an unusually strong aroma that humans are not used to. They are great sentient beings who are simply misunderstood. Zhirbaana had friends from Smetna and she thought they were wonderful. She once had a conversation with one and asked him, "Tell me, when you first came to our planet, did you think that humans had a strange odor, or smell, to them?" He replied, "Actually, yes! Yes, I did!" She said, "What did you think we smelled like?" He responded, "I think it is the smell of beef. I didn't know it at first, but I think that humans eat so much beef that that's what you smell like to us." She couldn't believe it, and said, "Really?" He said, "Yes." She continued, "That's very interesting, because your kind has a distinct odor to most humans as well." He looked surprised, and responded, "Really?" Zhirbaana couldn't believe he didn't know. She said, "Well, yes. Just like we may smell like beef to you, your kind sometimes has an aroma to us, which I can only guess is because of what you eat, too." He looked

PIXEL 5 – *Smellians (Continued)*

surprised.

Later, Zhirbaana's friend came to her and said he wanted help opening a business; they had a frank conversation. She said to him, "Do you remember our conversation about how humans smell like beef to you?" He replied, "How could I forget. It was an eye-opener." She continued, "Well, you need to understand that if you want to operate a business in this country, you are going to have to change some things." He said, "Like what?" She looked at him, trying to figure out how to answer in a gentle manner, so as not to hurt his feelings.

"Let me ask you. If I were to travel to your planet Smetna, and I opened a business, do you think that I would have difficulty because I smell like beef?" He looked puzzled, "Well, now that I think about it, you probably would. Most Smetnians abhor how humans smell … no offense!" She replied, "Oh, no … none taken. I'm glad you feel you can be so open and honest with me. But I have to tell you, that is how humans feel about Smetnians." His jaw dropped. "What?"

Zhirbaana interjected, "Look, you are wonderful beings, and I do not mean to offend you at all. I want you to be a great success in your new business, but you are going to have to change some things first." He sheepishly said, "Like what?" She continued,

PIXEL 5 – *Smellians (Continued)*

"Well, to be able to do business in this country, you have to observe proper human hygiene and etiquette protocols." He was befuddled and said, "What do you mean?" She explained, "You may need to change your dietary habits, use hygienic products, and learn how to relate to our society in common social circles. Look, you need to learn how to blend in to your community so that you not only fit in, but you are the role model for all others to follow within your community. If you stand out as an alien, you will never be accepted, and your business will fail. Do you understand?" He was silent for a moment, but quietly responded, "You are right. I never realized it before, but now I see exactly what you mean. I do need to make some changes." Zhirbaana suggested to him that he read a book called <u>American Ways</u>, which explained everything she was talking about in great detail and they concluded their meeting. Part of her felt bad about what had just happened, but deep within, she knew she had to tell him the truth, because she cared for him; she wanted him to succeed.

A month later, Zhirbaana's Smetnian friend showed up in her office, but he looked like a very different being. "Well, hello," she said, "It is great to see you!" He responded, "Likewise my friend!" He had a huge smile on his face, and he didn't smell like

PIXEL 5 – *Smellians (Continued)*

a "Smellian" anymore; he was even wearing cologne. In fact, he was dressed very fashionably for even a human. He said, "I cannot thank you enough for helping to open my eyes. Everything you told me was absolutely true. It was an eye-opener and I was upset at first, but we have a saying on our planet, 'When at Soluva, do as the Soluvians!'" She laughed, realizing the cliché. He continued, "What you taught me isn't just going to help me become a great success, I believe it is going to help my family survive in this world. I cannot thank you enough!" He clutched her and gave her a big hug.

To this day, Zhirbaana's Smetnian friend is not only a great business person, thriving in a challenging middle-class American community, he is also a great business role model for Smetnians from all over the galaxy.

How critical is proper hygiene and etiquette in the business world? If Zhirbaana had not shared her knowledge with her Smetnian friend, do you think he would still be in business today?

Chapter 6

The Dream

After returning home, I went back to my common servitude at Xamron. I had trouble sleeping, though. I experienced strange dreams. One evening, I dreamed about Xamron. I saw Xiggy in my dream, but I also saw something very disturbing. All of us, even the humans, had become robots. *We were operating according to the corporate systems, but we had no life.* Our customers were distraught and disorderly, even violent. They surrounded our building and shrieked out horrible things at us. I wanted to cry, but I couldn't. I was a robot. One customer threw a Molotov cocktail through the window and our office exploded with fire. We could not escape, but we stopped caring. We were lifeless. The fire alarm went off and the water sprinkler system kicked on. Water sprayed over the entire office, causing the fire to subside. But, the water started burning my metallic skin. "Oh my," I thought, "I'm metal. I'm rusting!" I looked around and I saw Xiggy, disintegrating before my very eyes into a pile of rust. All of us were. I cried out, in my robot voice, "No!" and I watched my body turn into rust. We were all just piles of rust, but I was still conscious. I lay there powerless, with no hope.

A sparkle appeared in the midst of the office. Though I had no eyes, I could see it. It grew into a bright white light, which took form. It was Farin, but she looked different. She was fierce, like a great blue screaming banshee. She floated above the debris and piles of rust.

Then she spoke, "Tell me; what do you see?" I couldn't speak, but I heard my own voice reply in a ghastly tone, "I see destruction … desolation." She asked, "Why?" My voice responded, "It is because our customers are angry with us. They hate us." She said, "And do you know why they hate you so?" I couldn't answer. She spoke, "It is because you do not love them. You do not truly care for them. You merely care for their money. They are a means to your paycheck. And because of this, you have become their enemy, whom they have destroyed." I said, "How could this have happened?" She answered, "You do not understand the way of passionate customer service. Answer this, who are the customers of Xamron?" I said, "It is the parents who pay for their children to receive the brain-chips." She said, "Is that all?" I couldn't answer. I didn't know how to respond. I was perplexed. She continued, "There are five levels of customers in your company. They have all suffered neglect. This is why you have been destroyed. It starts with the President." I said, "President?" She continued, "Yes, your President! He is the shining light for all to follow. His customers are the management and Vice-Presidents." I cried out, "That can't be. They are his employees!" She screamed, "No! You are wrong! He works for them. He must serve them first and be the great model for them to follow." I was shocked and confused. She went on, "The Vice-Presidents and management have failed in their customer service to the associates." I responded, "I don't get it." She said, "The Associates are their true customers. They were meant to serve them." "No," I cried, "We are their employees, their subordinates, their servants! We are not worthy! That cannot be right!"

Farin floated down to my pile of rust. She waved her wand and a flash of light enveloped me. I was whole again; I was human; I sucked in the breath of life once more. She stood before me and said, "Do you desire the truth, or not?" I hesitated, but after a moment of thought, replied, "I do." She said, "Listen, you must understand the true way of customer service, and regardless of whether you believe me or not, you must pay close attention to all I tell you, for it is truth." I nodded in obedience.

Farin continued, "Management exists to serve the employees. You had it wrong all the while. The Vice-Presidents and management must strive to see that the Associates are happy and doing well. They must love and treat them with great respect, putting them above their own selves. Those who seek the roles of power for power's sake do not deserve to rule." I stuttered, "But... but that's not how it has ever been? That cannot be!" She said, "Yes, that is truly how it is among the great corporations. But let me ask you, associate, who is your customer?" I shook my head, not knowing how to answer.

She said, "Your customers are the store managers. Tell me, how have you treated them?" I stammered, "I... I don't know." She shrieked, "Lies! You do know! Let me tell you! You do not love your store managers! You know their names, but do you know their families? Their friends? Do you know their dreams, goals, and desires in life? No! You do not! You are a selfish man and not

53

worthy of having them as your customers. This is why destruction has come upon you!"

I fell to the floor in shame. I quivered and coiled up in the fetal position, knowing all she said was true. But she continued in a quiet voice, "And, because you have not shown such glorious customer service to your store managers, they learned all they know from you. They modeled you. They treated their customers, the parents, with the same despicable customer service that you modeled to them. That is why their customers attack your office with derision, fire, and burning contempt. This is why Xamron is no more."

Then, I awoke.

Element 10 (E10): Identify all customer levels (Feature A). There is never just one level of customer that exists externally outside of the company. Employees are also "internal" customers who exist at various levels within the company. There are no "superiors" in a business. Determine who your true customer is for every level of management, starting with the President, as the president's internal customers are the VP's and upper management. Customer service must transition from a bland, two-dimensional, horizontal ideology to a vertical, three-dimensional level, penetrating every department, impacting all employees and associates at every level. Only then will proper customer service reach out and impact the external customer.

Element 11 (E11): Customer feedback. (Refer to Features C and D) Every level of customer must provide feedback and every associate must be evaluated by their direct customers, even all the way up to the President. This feedback is a primary factor in annual and mid-year evaluations. It is used to determine annual raises and bonuses.

Element 12 (E12): *Personal accountability. Do not expect others to do what you know needs to be done. Take it upon yourself and model it for them. Show them your exuberance and passion for your work. Decide to be the one who exudes greatness in your work. Become the epitome of greatness, because greatness competes with no one.*

PIXEL 6 – *Rinosceron Angst*

Lih was a young, new employee working for a portal package-delivery corporation; she worked under a manager from the planet Rinosceron. Lih exemplified many great characteristics as a young employee; none being greater than her ability to mirror her superiors. Unfortunately, her Rinosceron boss was a poor role model. Lih mimicked her new manager to the "T." Her boss, Bort, told her, "It doesn't matter what customers say! You don't need them; they need you! Don't take $#!+ from them! What you say goes!" Lih was trusting, and a bit naive, but she was a loyal employee. She did exactly as Bort told her.

Lih dealt with their customers exactly as Bort would. She was brash, brazen, and confrontational; she didn't know any better. Not long after, Bort, in his usual Rinosceron manner, plowed over one of their customers for questioning him publically. Lih thought Bort was amazing, but Bort did not remain in that capacity, for obvious reasons. Lih shed tears when she was told Bort was leaving. She idealized him.

After Bort's departure, a new manager, named Qirk, replaced him. Qirk was the absolute opposite of Bort. Lih despised him, though Qirk was professional, kind, and customer service-oriented. After he became her manager, Qirk realized how his

PIXEL 6 – *Rinosceron Angst (Continued)*

new employees, especially Lih, were quite "anti-customer-service" oriented. He was determined to change that.

Qirk called a team meeting immediately and introduced himself to his staff, "I am excited to be able to work with you; I consider it an honor to be your new manager. If I can help you in any way, my door is always open."

The team seemed pleased with their new manager after the meeting, that is, all of them except Lih. She thought he was fake and a "suck-up." Qirk realized quickly that Lih was going to be a challenge. He wanted to completely change the atmosphere of their office, so that customers would begin trusting them again. He knew that was the only way they were going to start becoming profitable. Until then, their business was in the red and his team didn't even realize that they were on the road to being shut down.

At other meetings, he asked his staff what their personal and business goals were. He recognized that most of their personal goals, in some way or another, related to making more money. He strategically linked their personal goals to the success of the business, saying such things as, "If we can become the top team in our company, and we generate the highest profits this year, we will get

PIXEL 6 – *Rinosceron Angst (Continued)*

better raises and bonuses; who knows, even promotions may be in store for us." He turned to each employee and said things like, "If that happens, Jor, you can get that new hovercraft you've been dreaming of. Lih, you could make enough to take your children on that dream vacation to the planet Uravia …" He opened their eyes so that they realized that their employer had the keys to giving them virtually all they wanted in life. Their excitement grew. Qirk explained further, "There is one important key to accomplishing this. We have to focus on improving our customer service drastically. We must change our mindset, our paradigm, so that we treat our customers better than anyone else. I don't know what you were told about customer service before, but we are here to serve our clients; they are not here for us. If we serve them well, better than anyone else, we will grow through great word-of-mouth marketing. Great customer service equates directly to profitability. It really is a matter of our survival; none of us are above being cut; no one is irreplaceable; if we do not become profitable, we could be downsized, or even our entire office shut down; don't think it can't happen; it does. I know, because I have seen it."

The team experienced a wake-up call. They began seeing their customers differently for the first

PIXEL 6 – *Rinosceron Angst (Continued)*

time, realizing that their customers' ultimate happiness could lead to their own. They were now all on board, that is, except for Lih. She still was not convinced.

A few days later, Qirk overheard Lih on the phone with a customer. She was very rude and short-tempered with the customer; she hung up on her; Lih was getting worse. Not long after, a different customer sent Qirk a long email about Lih, demanding that he terminate her immediately. Qirk called the customer and apologized to her profusely. He told her that the situation would be remedied immediately.

It was a Friday afternoon. Qirk called Lih into his office and told her about the complaint he had received. He said, "Lih, I like you and I think you have great potential. I want you to be a success in whatever you do, but it is not happening now. I will do what I can to help you become successful, whether it is here, or somewhere else. I want you to take the weekend to think about it. If you want to be successful here, you are going to have to change. You just cannot treat customers the way you do. If you cannot change, I will even try to help you find a job somewhere else, and maybe you can be happy and successful there, but it is up to you. By Monday, I want you to give me a plan about what you intend to

PIXEL 6 – *Rinosceron Angst (Continued)*

do."

Monday came and they had their fateful meeting. Lih didn't look like the same person; she was somehow different. She told him, "I realize … that you were right. I have been acting like an immature child and I need to change." Tears came to her eyes. She continued, "You have to understand, when I worked for Bort, I never really worked in the professional world before … that's how I thought you were supposed to treat people in business. Bort didn't respect customers at all … that's how I thought it was done. I promise you, I am going to do a complete 180; I'm going to change." And she did.

Qirk was relieved to hear her decision. From that moment forward, Lih became not only better at customer service, she became the best employee he had at it. Qirk had her attend customer service trainings, professional development courses, and business etiquette classes. Within a few years, she was one of the top employees in the company. Also, within that same period of time, their team finally made a profit. In the third year, they were honored nationally as the team of the year and they became the keynote speakers at their company's national conference.

PIXEL 6 – *Rinosceron Angst (Continued)*

How much do employees mirror their leadership? What strategy did Qirk use to save his office from being shut down? What do you think was the primary reason this business was failing before Qirk assumed management?

PASSION FORMULA

Chapter 7

Thermite

Did you ever have one of those days where everything just feels … you know … weird? Well, the next day I couldn't stop thinking about my strange dream and how true it was. It was disturbing. What happened next was also … unusual, to say the least.

I have a sixteen-year-old son who, like me, loves chemistry. He was walking through the living room carrying a plastic bag of some brown, powdered contents. I said, "What is that?" He responded, "It's iron oxide. You know … rust." I remembered the piles of rust from my dream; it struck a nerve. "Rust?" I asked. He said, "Yeah!" I continued, "So, what in the world are you doing with a bag of rust?" He answered, "I'm gonna' mix it with some powdered aluminum." I said, "Okay, and why would you do that?" He responded, "Well, it's really cool. Believe it or not, if you take something as worthless as rust and mix it with aluminum powder, which is also kind of worthless, you get a compound that is so powerful, it burns at 4000 degrees (f) and can burn through almost anything. It's awesome!" I said, "Really? What is it called?" He responded, "Thermite!"

At that instant, I had an epiphany. My dream came back to me and I saw Farin floating above the piles of rust. With a flick of her wand, I saw sparkling powdered aluminum light over the piles of rust. Reality came back to me; my son said, "The trick with thermite is, you have to use a burning piece of the element magnesium, or an intense flame, to light it. It's extremely hard to light, but once you do, it's impossible to extinguish. It's awesome!"

I drifted back into my trance, where Farin was waiting for me. She said, "You must become the torch. You must light these piles of rust and bring your company back from desolation. Be the intense flame; this is what you must become!"

"Dad?" my son queried, rousing me out of my daze. "Oh, sorry, son," I responded, "That is fascinating." He said, "Yeah, and do you know what else is cool? You can actually burn metal. Come here. Let me show you."

I got up and followed him outside. He reached into his pocket and pulled out a wad of iron wool. He dug into his other pocket and extracted a 9-volt battery. He explained, "It's amazing what you can do to something as worthless as a piece of old iron wool when you add electricity to it. Watch this!" He lightly touched the electrodes of the battery to the wool. A small spark ignited the metal and little sparks began to dance and flicker over every thread. Heat started growing and the iron wool was burning hot. It looked like a shimmering nebula. It was amazing and beautiful. I was mesmerized.

My thoughts drifted off; I saw Farin. She said, "There are those you work with, who are like this iron wool. They have been in your company for many years; they are rough, stubborn, and unchanging, much like the iron wool. They, however, are the metal that burns. You must ignite a spark in them. Shock them with your passion and energy. They can burn with passion. They may seem immoveable and indifferent, but you must touch them and ignite them with power, just as this battery has ignited this old iron wool. You must do something that shocks them out of their robot like apathy. Shock them in a positive way and they will burn with passion; it will be a beautiful sight to behold."

I drifted back to reality; my son continued, "What's really amazing about this reaction is that this is no longer plain old iron; it's iron oxide now." I interjected, "Do you mean the same iron oxide that can be used to make thermite?" He responded, "Yeah. Isn't that awesome? Now watch this! If you mix seven parts of this iron oxide with three parts of aluminum powder, you have thermite." He stirred the concoction and poured it into a steel pan, which was lying on a mound of sand. He handed me some sunglasses and said, "You might want to put these on. The light from thermite is as bright as the sun; it can damage your eyes." He set a torch flame to it; it ignited.

A flash. A burst of bright white light. The thermite was incendiary, powerful, and robust. We watched in awe, silently, considering the sheer power of such a simple elemental formula. It burned so hot that it melted through the steel pan and into the sand. I pondered, "How could two simple elements cause such a powerful reaction?" Farin's voice whispered in the deep recesses of my mind, "It is not the power of the elements, nor of the formula. It is the power of the spark, the small flame that creates the reaction within that which is inert and useless. Become that spark; become that small flame and your company will burn with great power and force; it will become thermite!"

Element 13 (E13): *Be the spark. Intensify your energy and passion within your company. Ignite all those you come into contact with. Excite and inspire. Let them feel your energy, even as you enter the room. Consider all those around you as inert elements that are waiting for an intense flame to ignite them. Be that flame. With patience, intensity, and confidence, you will cause your company to catch the fire of passion. Together, with your associates, as one corporate entity, you will amplify your powers; you will burn greater, brighter, and more powerful than thermite.*

PIXEL 7 – *Scorian Squietches*

Tradition has it that squietches first came to our planet centuries ago as hideaway parasites from a Scorian space cruiser. Scorians are known for a lack of cleanliness and poor standards. On their planet, squietches are common household bugs; some even joke and call them Scorian pets. The insects thrive in filthy, dark lavatories. Most humans hate squietches. No one saw them coming, and we have not been able to eradicate them since.

Because businesses commonly have beings from all over the universe frequent them, they have come to be known as safe harbors for squietches, especially their restrooms. One customer, Jaerla, compares the experience of entering into a local Quicky King restroom to that of being tortured in an Exhortian death pit. In other words, it is an excruciatingly disgusting and painful experience. Jaerla explains, "I am from a small space port, with only one fly-light intersection. Like most remote space-ports, we have a Quicky King. Everyone loves the Quicky King, because it really is the only fly-through hangout around. The only problem is that it is infested with squietches, mostly in the restrooms. Some locals don't seem to care, but I do. If I ever have relatives visit us from other planets, I always warn them, 'Stay away from the Quicky King restrooms! They've got squietches. In fact, I can't even go there anymore.

PIXEL 7 – *Scorian Squietches (Continued)*

It's downright nasty!'"

The reason so many establishments, such as Quicky King, have squietches is that they do not uphold standards, especially standards of cleanliness. They are franchised and regulated loosely; the franchisor finds it a challenge to control every independently owned and operated store. Often, the owners of the stores ignore how clean their restrooms are because they don't think it really matters. It also impacts their wallet. One owner, Larp, said, "I'm not a restroom service provider. My customers don't come here to use the restroom. They come here for the products we offer. Look, it's a waste of my resources to have to worry about how clean the restrooms are. Who cares? I can't have my employees going to the restrooms to check and clean out all the squietches every 30 minutes. It's costly and they've got better things to do." Larp is not alone in his stance. He considers himself a "big-picture" kind of guy, who doesn't have time to sweat the details. He concludes, "Hey, I'm a wealthy man, with lots of Quicky Kings. If people really cared about cleanliness and standards, how could I be so successful?"

Larp has an interesting viewpoint, but what he does not realize is that there is a large segment of customers who won't set foot in his stores, because

PIXEL 7 – *Scorian Squietches (Continued)*

of their lack of standards, customers like Jaerla. These are customers who would bring more business to Larp if he only maintained even minimal standards.

Jaerla said, "You know, Quicky King may think it is okay now to squeak by and provide substandard service, but you just watch, everyone knows that the only reason they are still open is because they are the only one in town. You mark my words, if any new competitor came to town, they would put 'Queasy' King out of business, without a doubt. You know, maybe I'll rally some of my friends and we'll open a … Fast Queen! That'll teach them!"

How important do you think standards of cleanliness are in business? If Jaerla opened her own business next to Larp's, who do you think would provide a better customer experience? How much do you consider this topic to be a matter of business survival?

Chapter 8

Emotibank Technology

After my son and I experimented with thermite, I went back into my house and sat down to watch some television. I have over one million channels, but it always seems like I can never find anything interesting to watch. I finally settled on a public service channel that had a fascinating documentary on Emotibank technology.

The narrator said, "… About a century ago, when sentient robots were first manufactured and sold commercially, they were unable to express emotions. That is, until one scientist, Dr. Zhaio Qinn, discovered a way to make them virtually human. He called it 'Emotibank' technology. Today, we refer to it as 'E-Tech.' This programming changed everything in regard to human/robot relations. Most of the robots that corporations purchase are usually programmed to have very low levels of emotional responsiveness; that way they are more controllable, but that is why they are rather apathetic and often do not seem to care much. There is a good side and a bad side to increasing emotional expressiveness in robots. If some corporate droids had a higher level of emotional response, they might potentially argue or even fight with customers.

"Some droids that are used for personal entertainment or companionship are intentionally programmed to express high levels of emotion. Those robots may literally cry, become angry, scream, or even grow so enraged that they get into fights. But, they can also synthetically

71

express happiness, kindness, or even love. On rare occasions droids have committed 'robocide' (i.e. suicide), by jumping off of buildings or by ripping out their own internal wiring and circuitry. It is a strange technology.

"One of the prime features of E-Tech is that it makes robots evaluate and grade the way they are treated in every situation. The robots store each negative or positive experience in their Emotibanks. Each Emotibank has a scale for measuring each experience. The worst negative experience is graded, for instance, a negative twenty; or the best would be graded a positive twenty.

"For example, a fast-food restaurant utilizes a droid as its front counter clerk. The robot speaks to a new human customer who has a disdain for robots. For no real reason, the customer is rude to the robot; she says, 'You better get my order right, you heap of scrap.' She also mumbles under her breath, saying, '… you worthless pile of junk.' Since the two have never met before, the droid generates a file, creating an imprint of the customer; the robot records the experience. The new experience starts out at a zero grade. After the experience is over, it is graded as a positive or negative. In this scenario, the robot scores the customer with a negative one. The next time she enters the store, the droid recalls her and expresses resentment towards her, by intentionally ignoring her as she stands at the counter. She yells out, 'Hello! Lug-nut! Are you dumb and deaf too?' The robot takes her order, but starts to grade her with a lower negative grade, which is programmed as the equivalent of revulsion, in human terms. This second encounter causes him to score her as a negative eight. This results in the droid gradually giving her worse and worse customer service, until she gets all the way down to negative twenty. At that point, the robot refuses to serve her, throws the food at her, or walks out and leaves. It can be quite humorous at times.

"In an interview, I asked Dr. Qinn why he sought to program robots to express such intense emotions. He explained, 'Practically everyone wants to be able to relate to their robots, but they can't. They want them to become more human, but they're not. The only way to make them more human-like is to use Emotibanks.' Later in the interview, I asked, 'What inspired you to invent E-Tech?' He responded, 'It's quite simple, really. I just analyzed humans and how they relate to people. I realized that internally, humans also score each experience they have with one another. When one meets a new person who is rude to him, deep in his brain, he unconsciously records and scores the experience. I call it an Emoti-Bank, because it is exactly like an 'emotional bank account.' If you treat a human kindly, it is like making a deposit into the bank. If you treat that person rudely, it is like making a withdrawal. If there are more withdrawals than deposits, you become bankrupt. That is how humans and E-Tech robots work. That is how humans can have them as companions … or even friends.

"'If you don't believe me, try this experiment. When you meet a new person or customer who you will likely have an ongoing relationship with, make a positive deposit into their psychological bank. Say something kind and uplifting to them; build them up; do something that makes them happy; give them a gift or treat. Think of that person as having an Emotibank; with each positive contribution, you are causing their Emotibank level to increase one grade. Now, after at least seven or so grade increases, intentionally do something negative toward them. You will see that they don't like it, and it will decrease your Emotibank a grade or two, but they will likely forgive you and will overlook your negligence or fault, though it is possible to wipe out your entire positive reserves with one strong destructive action. On the other hand, if you had started out the relationship with a negative experience, they will automatically despise you, because you are immediately at a negative grade level. That doesn't mean you will always remain at that level; it just means that you will have to try harder with multiple positive experiences to raise them up to a positive grade level. Emotions are gradable experiences and robots utilize similar programming to express synthetic emotions and responses. This is how Emotibank technology works.'"

After I watched the television program, I realized that really is how humans are, too. The doctor was right. Like robots, we have our own mental "Emotibanks." If people make negative emotional deposits, our brains, like Emotibanks, score them negatively and we treat them negatively. If they treat us nicely, they make positive deposits, which cause us to treat them well also. After watching that show, I determined that from that moment forward, I would strive to make only positive deposits into other peoples' lives, so I could become emotionally wealthy with everyone I encountered. Not everyone is able to become financially rich, but, by being nice to others, and by giving them positive deposits of kindness, we really can become rich in a way that impacts lives. And maybe, just maybe, that's the best kind of riches that a person can have.

Element 14 (E14): *Create positive experiences with your customers. The only negative experiences should be accidental, and scarce at that. If you have enough positive "experience deposits" with your customers, they will overlook any accidental negative "experience withdrawals." This is how you build an overall positive customer-experience relationship.*

PIXEL 8 – *Zed & Ot*

Zed and Ot are clones. In the future, to be politically correct, clones are referred to as, "para-siblings," because they are genetically parallel. Zed and Ot both work as interdimensional travel consultants. Obviously, they are virtually identical; they look alike, dress alike, and even work in the same office complex together. Strangely enough, their personalities, customer service philosophies, and people skills are as night and day. One independent analyst sought Zed and Ot out to investigate what made them so different in business. The analyst watched the clones in their interactions with customers. He noted that when Ot met a customer, he came across as very serious and businesslike. Ot was a no-frills kind of guy. His introduction was canned and expressionless, and it went like this, "Hello, my name is Ot. I understand that you would like to travel to the Ezorticza dimension. Let's look at the travel schedules and prices and see if any of them interest you." Ot did not technically do a bad job, but he came across as cold and unapproachable; his customer service skills were lacking. Zed was quite the opposite.

The analyst observed Zed as he was working with a new customer, named Sedge. Their meeting went like this, "Hello, my name is Zed, and you are…" "Sedge." "Well, Sedge, it is so nice to meet you.

PIXEL 8 – *Zed & Ot (Continued)*

Did you find your way here okay?" The customer responded, "Yes, I did, thank you." Zed said, "Great! Please come in and make yourself at home. Sedge, would you like coffee, tea, water, or a soft drink?" The customer responded, "Water sounds good, thanks." "No problem at all. Let me get it for you. I tell you what, would you like me to give you a little tour of our offices? I figure that if we are going to start a long relationship together, you might want to know where everything is and a little about where we came from. Would you like that?" The customer responded, "Sure, why not." Zed gave Sedge a complete tour of their facilities and he told him about their company's founder; he also gave him a brief history of how it all began. Sedge was fascinated as Zed continued talking about the company with excitement and vigor. He drew Sedge into his world, making him feel as though he was about to become a part of something greater and bigger than himself. Zed showed Sedge some of the industry awards they had received for being recognized as a top service provider in their field. He also shared some pictures of his happy customers and some of their quotes about how their service changed their lives. Zed also encouraged Sedge to tell him about himself, his family, and his travel aspirations. Sedge was utterly impressed and they had not even started looking at

PIXEL 8 – *Zed & Ot (Continued)*

travel schedules and prices yet. By this time, Sedge already wanted to do business with Zed and he liked him very much.

When the analyst asked Zed and Ot their customer service philosophies, Ot said, "Business is business. I don't waste my customer's time, just like I don't want them to waste mine. I figure that you get customers in and get them out. If they don't like what we have to offer, they can go elsewhere. It's a numbers game. Sure, I can spend a lot of time with each customer, catering to them, but at the end of the day the more customers I get in here and get out of here, the more sales I make. That's my philosophy."

Zed had a different take. He said, "I try to look at things from my customer's point of view. I treat them as I would my own family. You know, most customers have never travelled interdimensionally before, so they are a bit nervous about the whole thing. They don't really want just a quote, they want someone who can hold their hand and help them through the whole process; they need someone to empathize with them; that's what I do. I keep my customers, because they like the service I provide and they know they can trust me. It's all about those two things: service and trust. Some of my customers don't just come back to me for return business, they have become my close friends and they would never

PIXEL 8 – *Zed & Ot (Continued)*

dream of taking their business anywhere else. I think that the more quality time I invest in creating a great experience for my customers, the more my customers are willing to invest in me. They even tell their friends to come to me. I think my current word-of-mouth marketing is at 70% now; that's huge, especially in this industry! My customers are the best, and I really do love them; I mean it."

After Zed shared his philosophy, he said, "After I serve each customer, I send them an email asking them how well I performed for them. I ask them to send me their feedback so I can improve, and I give them my supervisor's email address, so they can contact him directly instead, if they want to. To date, I have not received one negative response. In fact, I find the feedback to be very motivating. It's exciting to know how much of an impact I have made in people's lives. It helps me to enjoy my work more every day."

Is it better for a business's brand to handle a high volume of customers with a low quality of service or to focus on a high quality of service with a low volume of customers? Why? Who do you think is the higher earning employee, Zed or Ot? Which employee better represents his brand for long term growth?

PASSION FORMULA

Chapter 9

The Queen Bee

I changed the channel. A news special about space bees was on; I decided to watch it for a while. Space bees are amazing creatures. Unlike earthly, insect-type bees, space bees are massive, intelligent creatures, with beautiful rainbow colored physiques. Their translucent wings actually refract light as they fly, causing the light to seemingly burst with all the colors of the spectrum. It's an amazing sight to behold.

As for the queen space bee, she's twice as large as a normal space bee, and twice a beautiful. Ask the typical person on the street what they think of a queen space bee and they will say, "Oh yeah, that's what I wanna' be like, the one in complete control … the boss! Yeah, that's the life for me."

The show's anchorperson explained, "The queen space bee, to the unlearned, appears to be the master of her destiny; the one completely in control; the goddess of the bees. The reality is, she is the servant of all. Though she is the object of glory for all who see her, she serves her hive as if she was its slave. In essence, it is the queen space bee's duty to provide for the hive. She must bear offspring, she must provide new workers, she must provide guidance and be the one who ultimately takes the blame should the hive fail and perish."

A televised interview with a real queen space bee followed; the queen said, "Look, everyone thinks it's great to be the boss-queen, the CEB, if you will. Truth is, I sometimes feel like a slave. I have to serve my employees, the drones and workers, and I have hundreds to please, not just one. Sure, it sounds glorious to be the queen bee, but it really isn't. I remember a time, when I was the new queen, where I had to pay my receptionist her weekly honey on a Friday afternoon, and I wondered how I was going to come up with the honey to feed my own family that night. Those were some tough days. Look, a true queen bee doesn't just have one boss to serve, she has hundreds. If I could start all over again, I might just choose to be a worker bee. At least they get to go home to their families after a hard day's work. I haven't seen my family in … weeks."

The reporter asked the queen bee what advice she would have for any young bee looking to be successful, maybe even as a future queen bee of her own hive. She responded, "Be happy in whatever you are doing, wherever you are. You don't have to be queen to be happy, or successful. In fact, it is a fallacy to want to 'be your own boss.' Often, I meet young bees just starting out who tell me, 'Someday, I want to be just like you! I want to be queen of my own hive!' I ask them 'Why?' They usually respond, 'I want to be in control!' or 'I want to be independent,' or 'I want to be the one in charge!' They are surprised when I ask them, 'So, do you think I'm in charge?' They reply, 'Well, yeah! Everybody knows that!' Then I share a little word of wisdom with them. I tell them that the reality is, no one is his or her 'own boss.' No one is 'in charge.' No one is 'independent.' Becoming Chief Executive Bee means you now have potentially hundreds or even thousands of bosses – the workers, drones, etc. and all of them come with great expectations about how you should perform. You are constantly being evaluated, scrutinized, and even ridiculed. Being queen isn't a full-time job, it's a 'sacrifice-your-entire-life, 24-hours-a-day, 7-days-a-week,' job. There is no such thing as personal time for a queen bee. You have to make tough decisions and sometimes good bees get hurt because of those decisions. When I announce a new policy, I do so knowing that it will cause some bees to become demoted, upset, or even terminated. It is not uncommon to receive anonymous death threats from disgruntled worker bees. So, is that the life you truly want? When I tell them that, they usually tuck their stingers and fly away.

I don't mean to dash anyone's dreams or discourage them. I just want everyone to realize that being a worker bee really isn't so bad. Everyone needs to strive to be content in whatever role they are given. They should buzz along with a song in their heart and consider how beautiful it is to be free to smell the flowers. That is something I haven't done since I was a baby bee. There are a lot of unrealized perks that come along with being a worker bee."

Element 15 (E15): *Be content. Be happy and successful in the role you are in. You may not be the CEO of your company, but determine the good aspects of your position and set your mind at being the best in it that you can be. Eliminate all negative thoughts; strive to be positive and uplifting to the associates around you. Life is short and every minute of it is precious, so don't waste one second of it moaning or yearning for what isn't or may never be.*

PIXEL 9 – *Bliss on Averocia*

Averocia is considered the most typical middle-class planet in the galaxy. Most of the inhabitants who live there are good, friendly, and hard-working aliens. It is a laid-back atmosphere; the residents like to focus on simple activities and home life, rather than pursuing trends and technological advances.

The Holophonix Corporation is a company that specializes in selling holographic phones and service contracts. Holo-phones are bio-digital contact lens devices that project a caller as a three-dimensional, realistic, life-sized, high-definition image within the user's retinas. The images are clear and look exactly like the person calling. If you speak to a person using holo-phones it looks and feels like he is in the same room with you. It is amazing.

Holophonix decided to open a store on the planet Averocia, but they did not expect tremendous results, considering the demographics. In fact, the demographics were slightly below average for one of their typical markets. They wanted growth, so they decided to take a calculated risk on the market. They recruited a lady named Trandy to open a store there. The manager who recruited Trandy described her as, "… a nice person who seems to have potential. She comes across as a bit reserved and maybe a little quiet. She is fairly professional. She may be a good fit for this market."

PIXEL 9 – *Bliss on Averocia (Continued)*

Trandy's store was in a fairly nice strip shopping center. Her business growth, however, over the course of three years was abysmal. In the length of time she was there, she only had between 65 to 70 service contracts running per month. It really was not enough to keep her doors open, but the company persisted.

After three years, Trandy had to resign, because her husband was being transferred in his job to another planet. The company decided to keep the store open and they found another lady to replace Trandy in her role. Her name was Bliss.

After Bliss had been operating the store a couple of years, the same manager who recruited Trandy described Bliss this way, "She is a ball of energy. She has great people skills and communication skills. Everyone who meets her loves her. She can talk to every type of person on their level. She is vibrant and excites people. Bliss is like … a cheerleader for our brand. When you are with her, you feel like you're at a pep rally with Holophonix as the home team. She makes everyone want to stand up and cheer for the team, even if they don't know anything about us. I have no doubt that her attitude and people skills are the reason for her great success."

Initially, on the outside, Bliss appeared to be much like Trandy; they even looked alike to some

PIXEL 9 – *Bliss on Averocia (Continued)*

degree. When Bliss assumed operation of the store, she stayed in the exact same facility, using the exact same equipment, and even the same staff. Nothing changed at all, except for the operator. But, then something miraculous happened.

Bliss started growing the business exponentially. Not long after she was there, they increased their monthly contracts by almost one hundred. But it didn't stop there. Every season after that, she grew by another hundred contracts per year, until she had approximately 900. Not only was it phenomenal for the market she was in, her growth was the highest that Holophonix had ever seen at any single store in the entire galaxy.

In hindsight, the Holophonix Corporation analyzed the situation to discern what had caused Bliss to be so successful. They considered the demographics, but the data was not exceptional. They considered the location, but it was average for one of their stores. They considered the marketing, but it was nothing beyond what they did in every market. They were also befuddled by the fact that the former operator had not achieved success there. The only difference they could discern was the change in operators.

PIXEL 9 – *Bliss on Averocia (Continued)*

What was the difference between the two operators? When Holophonix decides to expand into new markets, should they be more concerned about demographics, site selection, or the type of operator? What specific traits and skills should they look for in an operator in order to have more successful stores?

PASSION FORMULA

Chapter 10

Zombots

The future of the human race has turned out to be quite strange, but wonderful. Mankind has discovered how to overcome most calamities, in terms of war, disease, and believe it or not, even death. But there are a number of people who don't really care for the alternatives offered. I don't blame them.

If you want to cheat the Grim Reaper in the future, for the time being, the only way to do so is by either having your cognitive faculty transferred into a robotic body/host, either biologically or digitally. This means that you are alive, but you are no longer entirely human. Often, these robotically preserved people are given a rather derogatory name, "Zombots." This is not without good reason.

According to psychological studies, humans who have been transferred cognitively into anything beyond their biological human bodies often experience a gradual dehumanization. Not only do they physically become another entity, their own perception of themselves becomes warped to such a degree that they outwardly act lifeless, or zombified; hence the name Zombots.

Sadly, in my culture, Zombots are treated with little demand in the workforce, though the ones I know are really nice people. I have a colleague, Bruno, who works for a franchise company and unlike traditional franchisors, they primarily recruit Zombots. I asked him why. Bruno said, "Look, Zombots usually have difficulty obtaining jobs in the workplace, because they don't fit in, and they often have older cognitive faculties, because their human bodies grew too old to function. But they are usually people with large reserves of cash. That's how they can afford to undergo the operation to become a Zombot. They have no clue how to run a business, but they are fairly trainable. They need something to do for the rest of eternity, so we give them the chance to own their own franchise. Then, once they sign the Franchise Agreement, POW, they belong to us! We've got them for a 50-year contract, they've given us half a billion dollars for the franchise fee, and they can't do anything about it. Zombots are better than regular franchisees or employees, they're practically slaves!"

I thought his response was horrible. I couldn't believe that people actually thought that way. And, it was obvious that his company reaped what it sowed. I became so angry that I almost punched him. I blurted out, "Now it all makes sense. I now understand why your company is plummeting down the black hole of financial ruin. I can't believe you!" He was shocked at my response and said, "What do you mean? We're in the black! What are you talking about?"

I retorted, "You really can't see it? Your company's success is proportionally related to how you treat your franchisees. If you see them as mere employees, or slaves, they will only do what they must do at a bare minimum, but they will be resistant at every turn. You think you are creating indentured franchisees, but you are creating an army of rebels. You think you are creating a great empire on the backs of human-flavored machines, but these are real people, with real hopes, dreams, and desires. You are creating your own demise!"

Bruno said, "Relax, man! It's no big deal! Come on … besides, they're not really fully human, they're mostly machines with nothing else to do with their lives. At least we give them something to do with their miserable existence." I became so enraged, I blacked out …

I don't know what happened next, or how much time had elapsed, or how we got where we were, but I came to, standing on a hover-pod, over Bruno, who was lying prostrate and unconscious on the floor of the pod. "Oh, my goodness," I exclaimed, kneeling down to check on him. "Bruno! Are you okay?" He started to move, coughing, as he rolled over on his back. He had a black eye. "Oh my! What happened to you?" He said, "I … I don't know. One second we were talking and the next … I don't know. Where are we?" He stood up, and paused to look around. After a moment, he said, "Hey, we're at one of my stores … and look, there's one of my Zombots now." She was a gold metallic-looking woman who was standing behind a register.

We were hovering a couple of stories above the franchisee's store. The hover-pod was equipped with an audio/video surveillance system designed for evaluating franchisees, so I said, "Hey, it looks like she's working with a customer now. Can you turn this on so we can listen in to how she is doing?" He said, "Sure," and flipped on the camera and audio.

The screen, fuzzy at first, tuned in to the franchisee, who was talking to a female customer. The customer appeared to be completing her transaction and she asked,

"… I have one more question. Is this a franchise?" The owner said, "Technically … yes." The customer laughed and replied, "Technically? It either is or it isn't, right?" The store owner continued, "Look, it may be a legal franchise on paper, but it is nothing short of contractual imprisonment. Heck, if I were a slave, that might be a step up!" The customer was surprised, "Really? Wow! I never would have guessed. These stores are everywhere. I would have thought it was a great business to own." "Well, you thought wrong. There is no 'ownership' about it. They treat us like prisoners and they don't give a care about us at all. Take my advice and run as far away from it as possible. The product is good, but the franchise part of it is unbearable." The customer responded, "Come on, it can't be that bad. If it's so bad, then why don't you leave?" She replied, "How? With a 50-year-term, property lease, and no legal way to terminate without another half-billion dollars in penalties, I'm stuck. But, I'm not going to just lay back and take it. We franchisees are secretly doing something about it. Yeah, it is probably going to bring our company down to the ashes, but a defunct, bankrupt company has no power to enforce its early-termination penalties against thousands of angry franchisees. I promise you, we will be free of this tyranny, and we will crush every one of our slave-masters! I swear to god!"

I looked over at Bruno, and his jaw had dropped to the floor. "I can't believe it," he said. I shook my head and said, "You better believe it! I don't want to say I told you so, but …" He was silent; he looked up, confused, and he stared up into space. I waited for a moment, to let his new reality sink in. He had just plunged into the rabbit hole and was lost in a new wonderland of reality; one which he had never seen before. I knew he was having a hard time believing it all.

I broke the silence, "Look, Bruno, maybe this isn't such a bad thing that just happened. Think of it this way. Now that you know the truth, you can fix it before it's too late. You can be the hero … the savior for your company." I began to become excited for him. I continued with fervor, "Bruno, if you take this newfound information back to your company and shed the light of truth to all your executives and employees, maybe it's not too late to change your policies and create a new atmosphere of excellent customer service for your franchisees. You could turn this monstrous behemoth around and give these franchisees new hope and a new passion for life. If you make them love your franchise, instead of hate it, who knows what kind of profits and great success your company could achieve. Your word-of-mouth marketing would grow tenfold. Everyone would find a new take on what it means to be a franchisee. It could impact all society. Imagine it! You alone could change the entire world!" I stopped to catch my breath, as the zeal and thrilled expectation of new hope enveloped me.

I looked over at Bruno and realized that he was staring at me like a deer in the headlights. He responded, "What are you talking about? This just makes me realize that we aren't monitoring these ungrateful Zombots close enough. We need to tighten our reins and be tougher. Why, these sniveling, worthless…"

I don't recall much of what Bruno said after that. My head started spinning again and I blacked out…

Franchise Elements

Element 16 (E16): *If you are a franchised company, always remember that your franchisees are not your employees. Franchisees are your customers at every stage and phase of your relationship, from the point of initial inquiry until retirement.*

Element 17 (E17): *Increase the customer experience. After franchisees sign a Franchise Agreement, their positive customer experiences should intensify, not decrease.*

Element 18 (E18): *Cure the Cure. Bear in mind that the "Cure Letter" is not always the "Cure." Consider this; would you threaten to sue a new customer you just met? No, you would not, unless you had self-destructive tendencies. Therefore, why would you threaten a faithful customer you have built a long-lasting relationship with, who has helped you build your business for many years? Such a franchisor might need a cure to save themselves from bankruptcy. Always use Cure Letters as a last resort, because often such heavy-handedness may cause greater legal problems down the road.*

PIXEL 10 – *Y-Knots*

Ixsa is an extremely successful business alien. He is also a successful artist who enjoys strong profits from his surreal, futuristic artwork. An intergalactic online news reporter, named Onimo, conducted a story on Ixsa in effort to learn the secret of his success.

When Onimo entered Ixsa's private office, she was amazed at all the fantastic designs and works. His walls were black and red; multi-colored lights were everywhere. She said, "Wow, this is amazing … all the lights." He responded, "Yes, I have all the spectrum of the rainbow so that I am able to create the sensation of real light. It makes my art come alive." Onimo looked at one wall and saw a large rope with a knot tied in it. One end was unraveled so that it was in the shape of a, "Y." It was featured on a plaque, as if it was an award that had been presented to him; it had the inscription, "Y-Knot?" Pointing to the knot, she asked, "If you don't mind my asking, what is that?" He smiled with a huge grin and said, "That's my 'Y-Knot!'" She said, "I see. What does it mean?"

Ixsa explained to her, "I put that there to remind me of how I should treat my customers." Onimo looked confused, as he continued, "Let me explain. Many years ago, I used to be rather difficult in my approach with how I treated customers – not just customers, but people in general. When someone

PIXEL 10 – *Y-Knots (Continued)*

asked me to do something, I always looked for a way out of it. I was lazy, I guess. Really, I think it was more than that; it was a bad habit that I let develop over time. I got into this pattern of saying 'no' to everyone about everything, for no real reason. I didn't want to deal with any more than I had to; I was always, 'too busy," I would tell people. This caused others to keep me at a distance. I wouldn't go out of my way for them, so when I really needed something, they weren't there for me either. I don't blame them. I had become selfish and self-serving. I got to where I did not like people anymore. Something had to change.

Then, one day, I was talking to a customer who asked me to go out of my way to do something for him. Normally, I would have said 'no,' but on this day, I felt different, so I said, "Why not?" I went out of my way to achieve something for him that was not necessary and it didn't benefit me at all. But, because of it, later he introduced me to some more customers and my business sky-rocketed. I then realized that if it wasn't for that 'Why not,' moment, I wouldn't be where I am today. That is why I have a plaque with a "Y-Knot." I put it there to remind me at all times that if a customer asks me for something, I ask myself, 'Why not?'

"I have even taken it one step further. When I sense that a customer has a need or desire, I challenge

PIXEL 10 – *Y-Knots (Continued)*

myself to say, 'Why not help him?' or 'Why not surprise him with something?' I love to see their eyes light up when they realize that I went above and beyond for them, for no apparent reason at all. It makes them feel special, and you know what? It makes me feel good about myself. Once I adopted the 'Y-Knot' attitude and philosophy, my business turned into a complete success. Here, I want you to have one … it's a little something for you to remember me by. Why not?" Then Ixsa reached into his pocket, pulled out a miniature "Y-Knot," and he gave it to Onimo.

What did Ixsa do that caused him to experience a new realization? From this realization, what did he learn that changed the way he conducted business?

PASSION FORMULA

Chapter 11

The Brain Cell

The next morning, my phone rang; I awoke. I was lying in my den and I had no idea how I got there. Sadly, a friend had called to say that Bruno never made it home the night before and was reported as missing. I couldn't believe it. I can only guess that we had both been victim to some strange cognitive-disrupting radiation or phenomena that caused us to black out and lose our memories. Maybe Bruno never recovered from it and just wandered off into the darkness and was lost, never to return. No one will ever know. Poor fellow; we will miss him.

Anyway, after observing his franchisee's personal experience with his company, I took some time to reflect on how franchisors often treat their franchisees. Moreover, I considered how all businesses in general treat their customers as a whole. I entered into my "Brain-Cell." A Brain Cell, if you are wondering, is a special chamber designed to eliminate all distractions, while it electrically stimulates neural activity. It helps me to reach heightened levels of clarity and complete illumination.

After activating the machine, I saw amazing multi-colored flashes of light; a feeling of total peace enveloped me; my mind was completely lucid. My brain flourished with thought. I thought back to the elements. I realized that those elements are critical in developing a positive customer experience formula for every business.

I thought of all the ways of the universe and I began to consider the laws of physics. I recalled that in physics, there is a known law that teaches us that all things tend toward chaos. More specifically, it is the second law of thermodynamics, which states that the entropy of an isolated system never decreases, because isolated systems always move toward thermodynamic equilibrium: a state with maximum entropy. Let me explain.

Business systems are self-contained, isolated systems, and yes, even physics applies to them. Such systems *always* tend toward decay, unless they have massive amounts of the *right* energy injected into them to keep them from entropy, which is gradual chaos. In the business world, chaos is tantamount to failure. Often, businesses do inject huge amounts of energy into projects and systems, just like the planet Pendulum, but they are exerting the wrong kinds of effort.

There is a fundamental key that every business should observe in order to experience greatness. The *success* of every business *lies in the details*. I was inspired to carry that phrase as my banner because of a company that most everyone knows and loves; that company is Hershey's.

I thought about how, one day, I was in a convenience store looking at all the various confections. I do not recall why, but I picked up a large box of Hershey's chocolate bars and I looked at the bottom of the box. It read something to the effect, "This product left our factory in *perfect* condition. If it arrives in anything other than *perfect* condition, return it immediately." I was amazed and thought, "Wow! Perfection! Whoever thought of setting perfection as a standard?" It made me to understand that a business must seek perfection in all its endeavors.

I also recalled another epiphany, which changed my way of thinking. It was in regard to the term, "Intelligence." I remembered how I was once taught that, "Intelligence is the ability to make finer distinctions." From these two teachings, I came to my realization that true *success lies in the details*. To reach perfection, we must exert greater intelligence in paying careful attention to the minute details, the finer distinctions, of all we do in business.

From this philosophy, my brain swirled with enlightenment, until I conceived the Customer Experience Formula, which takes into account the finer distinctions of perfect customer service. It was a simple formula, but ingenious, and much like thermite is made from simple elements, this customer experience formula was produced from simple elemental concepts, though its power is just as explosive.

What I realized is that most businesses operate based on systems and processes to generate revenue, just like Pendulum, but they lack exceptional customer service, which is the primary factor to great business growth. I realized that general customer service in this day and age is the worst it has ever been in the history of our galaxy. Most employees and franchisees are not trained in how to communicate and deal with customers. Our business mentality has changed from that of a clerk saying, "Thank you for your business," to that of the customer feeling pressured to say, "Thank you for your service," while the clerk nods them off, looking annoyed at the fact that the customer took the time to bother them. When a customer enters a store, rarely do we hear, "Hello! We are so glad to

have you. How are you doing today?" or, "Great morning
to you! How may I serve you?" Our business industry
has evolved from customer-service to employee-service.
Mind you, I do understand that employees deserve to be
served well, with professional care, but they should not be
treated with any greater care than the customer.

How often do customers enter business establishments
where a clerk ignores them or makes them feel
uncomfortable for the "intrusion," because the clerk was
busy texting a friend?   How often do patrons attempt to
get a napkin or salt package from a clerk at a fast-food
restaurant, but they are treated as a nuisance? These are
not uncommon occurrences and I'm sure we can all relate.
There are so many poor customer-service stories that we
have all experienced, that I have no doubt each of us could
write volumes on such accounts. This realization is quite
saddening to me.

I then comprehended that the true fallacy today is the
opinion among the business masses as to what real
customer service is. Customer service is not merely
saying, "How may I assist you?," or "Thanks for your
purchase!" Such terminology is merely a veneer for
customer relations. Now, I ask you to take note of what I
am about to say, as this is the most critical point of my
realization. Mark it, highlight it, or tattoo it to your
forehead. Do whatever it takes to remind you of this at all
times. Perfect customer service does not specifically have
to do with what *you* say, or even do; it has to do with what
the customer *feels*, because of what you say and do. Perfect
customer service is entirely based on *what the customer
emotionally experiences through your actions*. That is it. This

is the finer distinction regarding intelligent customer service.

Any customer who enters your store with a glum countenance must leave your store with a smile on his face, or a chuckle in his heart. Customers must experience something memorable through their encounter with you that evokes a stimulating, positive, emotional response. If this is not the case, I can almost guarantee you that your business is suffering from entropy, and friend, entropy left to its own devices always wreaks a path of destruction and it always wins. It's physics, plain and simple.

Element 19 (E19): *Chaos destroys business. Without diligent care and effort, businesses tend toward decay. You must inject massive amounts of the right energy into them to keep them from entropy, which equates to gradual chaos and destruction.*

Element 20 (E20): *Success lies in the details. Always remember that "Intelligence is the ability to make finer distinctions." We must exert great intelligence in paying careful attention to the minute details, the finer distinctions, of all we do in business.*

Element 21 (E21): *Make perfection your standard. To achieve great success, a business must seek perfection in all its endeavors.*

Element 22 (E22): *Strive to achieve exceptional customer service. This is the primary factor to great business growth.*

Element 23 (E23): *Create emotional experiences. Perfect customer service relates to how the customer feels about what you say and do. Impeccable customer service is entirely based on what the customer emotionally experiences through your actions.*

Chapter 12

The Customer Experience Formula

I may appear to be against systems or processes, but nothing could be further from the truth. I am probably the most process-oriented person you could meet. I do adamantly believe that every business must have systems and processes in order to run like a well-oiled machine, but what I am fervently opposed to is the idea that one merely needs systems and processes to make the machine go. That is absolutely not true. The machine must have fuel, and that fuel can only come through exceptional, passionate customer experiences. Such experiences not only spur more customer growth, they fuel employees and give them something positive to look forward to every day.

Consider this: When a customer is emotionally stimulated, it is a moving experience for the employee as well. If an associate can make a customer excited, it is contagious and it makes others in the workplace happy. Positive emotional customer experiences are fluid and flow through everyone in a business. They generate good will and happy feelings among all, thus causing less complaints and negativity. In all, they are productive and profitable for everyone.

So, how does one create a world of such perfect customer experiences? He must diligently create an atmosphere of perfect customer service, where associates inspire one another to spark affirmative experiences to not merely affect the customer, but to *infect* the customer.

Infectious customer service is viral. It generates great word-of-mouth marketing, and through such growth, it changes lives and ultimately the world as we know it.

The Customer Experience Formula stands like a three-legged stool. If any one of the legs is missing, it will topple and fall over. Following are the three elements in the Customer Experience Formula:

Ce1 - Customer Experience Training – Such training must be conducted for all associates at every level. Every office/team/dept. must be trained in person by a customer experience expert. If you do not have a customer experience expert, hire one, or train someone from within your company to be your Customer Experience Manager. There must also be consistent online/video staff trainings held; customer experience training must always be a prime focus at any and all meetings.

Ce2 - Personal Accountability – Consistent and regular feedback (Features C and D) must be solicited from every internal and external customer at all levels (i.e. Feature A), as previously mentioned. This is accounted for in all personnel evaluations and is a key factor to raises/bonuses and promotions. Modify evaluation forms and processes to be heavily weighted based on results received from all customer feedback. Enforceability of element Ce2 is extremely critical.

Ce3 - Intense Expectations – Your staff will not know how to grow if you do not intensely express and model perfect customer experiences and case studies for them. If you ask for great sacrifice, they will give it, in terms of excellent customer service. They must be shown and told that we desire associates who convey a "full-life" commitment, rather than a "full-time" one. Let it be clear that I do not merely refer to time, in terms of hours spent, but to the *quality* of the time associates invest in working with customers. It would be better for associates to intensely invest their full-life working part time than for them to poorly spend part of their life working full-time.

When Ce1, Ce2, and Ce3 are combined, you have a living, breathing formula for explosive business growth and achievement. Companies that utilize this formula corporately will achieve business growth and renewal. Individuals who apply these principles to their own lives will also achieve renewed vigor and personal growth, even if their employers have not yet implemented the formula. It is impactful and contagious; it will change the world of business as we know it.

PASSION FORMULA

Chapter 13

The Passion Plan

As I sat in the Brain Cell, inspirations were overwhelmingly flooding my mind. But, I wanted more and more. I increased the neural-induction settings of the machine to the highest levels; my mind virtually exploded. It was as though I was in another dimension of time and space. Mentally, I was in a realm I had never experienced before. I was elated, in awe, staring into the infinity of my mind with boundless elucidation.

Then I saw it. It was the ultimate plan for supreme customer service. It would revolutionize the business world and create miraculous customer experiences all over the universe. It was thermite. The word "PASSION" bursts before my eyes, and a one-year-plan for initiating the ultimate customer experience model for businesses unfurled, like a majestic, royal banner.

It was a revelation, a new paradigm that all businesses striving for excellence would implement. I saw the twelve tenets of the plan laid out before me point by point, written as if it were a creed or doctrine. It specified:

I.   I resolve to become an impassioned customer experience expert.

II.   If I have the authority, I will appoint a Customer Experience Manager within my business. I will grant this person power to oversee and fulfill this plan.

III.   If I do not have the authority, I will volunteer to assume the role of being a "Customer Experience Coordinator." To model true customer service to my colleagues, dedication, and a full-life commitment, I will fulfill these duties along with my normal position. I will continue to do my expected duties without requiring additional pay raises/bonuses, etc. I will be available whenever and wherever needed.

IV.   I will establish a Customer Experience Committee (CEC) among my peers. This team will act as our "Brain Cell," to assist in creating and developing superior customer experience strategies for our company.

V.   As the Customer Experience Manager/Coordinator, I will develop customer experience and motivational trainings for our associates.

VI.   I will visit every team/department to conduct customer experience trainings from all that I have learned in this book.

VII.   I will create customer experience webinars/video modules for ongoing training for associates in remote offices/locations.

VIII.   With the guidance of the CEC, I will develop feedback forms for staff, management, executives, etc.

IX.   I will assure that customer feedback is to become part of my company's annual evaluation process. Any negative feedback will be handled by each associate's respective manager or by the CEC.

X. External and internal supplementary trainers will be utilized when needed.

XI. Customer service/motivational books/videos/tools will be provided to all associates.

XII. I will ensure that this program has the full and complete support from the president down to every level of management to succeed.

I gasped in amazement at the plan that was spread out before me. I thought, "This is absolutely amazing! I can't believe it! Truly, anyone following this grand recipe is bound to achieve phenomenal customer service." I spoke, "Brain Cell, transfer all these thoughts and ideas into a written format, so that it may be published and shared with the entire universe to see." The Brain Cell replied, "Data transfer commencing immediately."

After the data was transferred, without even packing, I hurried to the nearest intergalactic space station. I boarded the craft, leaving immediately to a distant galaxy, called Presidaion. I shared my vision with the Board of Universe Leaders; the Prime Executive ordered me, "We have seen into the depths of your mind and have been enlightened to this new truth. This board is in complete agreement regarding what you must do next. This revelation must be published for all living sentient beings to read. Once published, your first mission is to take your book to the planet Pendulum, for it is on the brink of complete and utter destruction. You must take an extensive journey, but this is the only hope we have to save them; not only them, this may be our only chance to save our entire business universe from cosmic annihilation. The realm of customer service as we know it is on the brink of widespread extinction. This is our only hope! Go now, and complete this mission set before you. Be steadfast and diligent; do not let anything stand in your way. You must get this book out to Pendulum and to every business in the universe … before it is too late!

FEATURES

PASSION FORMULA

Feature - Pixel Explorations

Pixel Exploration 1 - *Space-Fly*

In this Pixel, it is fairly obvious that the owner of Space-Fly is experiencing financial problems, because she is rarely at her store to serve new customers. She is basically an "absentee-owner." In essence, this equates to, "absentee-profits." The percentage of an owner's time that he/she invests into the business is usually directly proportional to the percentage of profit growth. Yes, absence makes the heart grow fonder, but it also makes the cash flow flounder.

In my business adventures, I often meet people who want to be their own boss, so they can enjoy the easy life. They imagine they will be sitting on a beach sipping margaritas while their business runs itself. That is a fallacy. 90% of success in business is just being there.

A new business is like a newborn baby. Just as a fetus has to complete a gestation period, a new business must undergo a research and training period, prior to being born. It is like an oak tree. It must first bear deep roots and gain a grasp on the soil before it can plunge its stem upward into the sky.

Like a newborn, the infant business requires constant nurturing and attention. It is not like a 9 to 5 job. It is a full-life job. Like a baby, you have to monitor your new business at all times. You have to watch him, feed him continuously, and even clean him up when he becomes soiled. Your new baby business will keep you up at night, crying out for attention. You cannot leave your infant business in the hands of strangers during business hours and hope that he will develop properly. Just as there is no "absentee-parenting," there is no true, "absentee-ownership." Successful business owners invest their lives into developing their new business until it has become an ultimate success. Then, once they have mastered the art of business-parenting, and their child has grown several years, they can train someone else to be their business's nanny. But the owner must never do so unless they are absolutely sure that their nanny loves and cares for their business as much as they do. As that child grows and blossoms, the owner can bear other newborn baby businesses that he can nurture and wean in a similar fashion.

The business owner who raises his baby businesses in such fashion can one day retire, knowing full well that the young businesses he fathered will one day grow up and take care of him in his golden years.

Pixel Exploration 2 - *Call of the Alien Worms*

Immediate response. These two words sum up the future of customer service. Those who carry these words as their banner will control the business realm.

I grew up in what I call the "Nintendo generation," or the "fast-food generation." Unlike my father, who enjoyed moseying down old country roads while looking out the window to watch cows and such, I never had much patience for that type of life. I was taught that "patience is a virtue," and I strived to be a patient person, but the reality is, people do not like to be patient. It is not in our nature. Why? It is because our days and hours on this planet are severely limited, and we don't want to waste one precious second waiting, simply because someone does not respect our time. And what is time? It is the amount of life we have left. If you don't respect a person's time, you do not respect his life.

In my career, I was trained that you should return customer calls within 24 hours or less, but I greatly disagreed. I abhorred that standard, because in reality, no one wants to wait for another person to answer them a day later, especially when they want or need something. I rebelled and held up a new banner, "Immediate response!" There is no reason to have any other standard; actually, there is another reason. It is called sloth.

Yes, I may seem passionate about this issue, but in the business world, this aspect of customer service is a critical matter of survival. Consider this: In this Pixel, the woman had an urgent need to have the alien worms exterminated or her home would soon be eradicated. One may say,

"Sure, I see her dilemma, but it's not like that in my business. What I offer is not a matter of life and death, or property destruction. There is no reason a customer can't wait until I respond." To that, I would say, not true, my friend, you are living in a make-believe world of unicorns and candy rainbows. True, it may not be a matter of your customer's life and death, but it is a matter of your business's life and death.

Your customers' need may not be as urgent as in the alien worm scenario, but their desire for getting what they want *immediately* is. One could rewrite this case study and instead of her desire to locate an exterminator, it could be to find a store that sells vacuum cleaners. The research process for vacuum vendors would be exactly the same. She would go to the internet and run a search for vacuum stores. She would call them and if she got a voicemail, she may or may not leave a message. She may call another, and if she cannot understand the receptionist, due to poor communication skills, she would hang up. She may call several, but the first person to answer her call and help her wins. The last vendor may say, "Would you like me to bring a few of our vacuum models to your house? I'd be glad to show them to you and give you a free demonstration. I'll even vacuum your home for you for free. I can be there within 30 minutes." That vendor's immediate response is why he will win the business game.

By the time this vendor has gone to her house, conducted a demonstration, and sold her a vacuum, the first business she called may not have even received her voice message, because he follows the "return calls within 24 hours" policy. But even if he does get her message within a few hours and calls her, she will not answer the call, because she has already given her business to someone else. He may leave her a message, but she will never call him back. He will always wonder why, but we know the truth. The first to provide an immediate response wins.

Pixel Exploration 3 - *Fizzy Parties*

We live in the era of the "do-it-yourselfer." When I was a child, virtually everything we purchased was pre-assembled. Ah, those were the good old days; we took it for granted. Unfortunately, all good things must come to an end. At some point in the evolution of the business industry, some ingenious sadist discovered that if a business only manufactures and packages a product, he would save money by eliminating assembly lines and lowering shipping costs, due to smaller packaging. This allowed him to sell his products at a lower price, thus giving him the ability to crush his competition. What a very wealthy and cruel man he was. Being a native Texan, I would only have one thing to say about a man like that – "Get a rope!"

Seriously, though, the transition of commercial products into those requiring assembly may seem to many to make businesses more money, but I would challenge that assumption. As the human race grows to become more leisure-oriented and financially better off, they don't want to spend their precious lives trying to find a missing screw; nor do they desire to assemble a product, and disassemble it numerous times, because they realize they attached a part backwards or left something out.

If a person wants to buy numerous products for his patio from a do-it-yourself store, he may have the money to purchase many items, but because he cannot spend his time assembling every item he wants, he will only buy a few. Otherwise, it would take weeks to assemble everything. People's time is becoming more valuable to them nowadays. Therefore, they would rather pay more for someone to do the work for them, rather than try to figure out how to become the manufacturer's free assembly-line worker. Face it: You will either pay for a product with your money or your time; which one is more valuable to you? You can always make more money, but you cannot make more time. Time is the most valuable commodity we have.

It would be wise if businesses sold their "assembly required" items along with some that are pre-assembled, yet at a higher premium. This would allow customers to make the decision about what they would rather spend, their money or their time.

In this case study, the clerk really did tell the customer that the product was hard to assemble, and he knew it, because he had bought one. The business owner has no clue that his employee is shooing customers off by sharing his own personal testimonies about the store's products. The clerk may as well hang a sign around his neck with the words, "Don't buy here!" If the owner knew what his clerk was telling customers, he might want to get a rope, too. But that is the way it is with businesses controlled by absentee-owners. Great sacrifices in quality customer service are made, though they should not be.

What is the better customer service solution? Many employers are negligent in wasting their capital by hiring non-productive employees. Often, clerks stand around at the cash register texting their friends or surfing the internet when they are experiencing slow business periods. If the store sells any products requiring assembly, the employees should assemble them when they are experiencing down-time. And, they should sell them at the same price as unassembled products. Why? Because this causes a better customer service experience. It gives the business an edge over its competition, guaranteeing more sales. After employees have assembled a few of the items, they are able to do it quickly without error. In the real case study, that is exactly what the second store did. Their managers assembled their products at no extra charge and the clerk mentioned that they were really fast at it. They went the extra mile for their customers, and that is why the clerk could boast that they were the number one store.

What should be learned from this Pixel is the psychology behind what the managers did when they decided to assemble the products for their customers for free. One manager was not just there to earn a paycheck, he observed his customers' buying habits and reactions to the products, so that he could increase their chances for success. Truly, success is in the details.

One day, this manager saw a little old lady, with shaky hands, looking at the product's box. She turned to the manager and said, "How in the world could that fit in this box?" He responded, "Oh, ma'am, that's because it is not assembled." She said, "You mean I have to put it together myself?" "Yes, ma'am." She blurted out, "Ah, poppycock! I can't do that. Do you have any that are already put together?" He replied, "No, but I tell you what. If you buy it, I'll assemble it for you later today on my break, and you can pick it up tomorrow. Would you like that?" The lady was ecstatic. She threw her hands up in the air and said, "You would do that for me?" He responded, "Absolutely!" She could not believe it, and she told him,

"Young man, you just made this my favorite store. From now on, I only do business with you!"

The manager shared his experience with the owner and they created a new policy to assemble all of the items when they were experiencing down-time. It revolutionized their business and their profits grew.

The point to be made about this Pixel is that employees must be trained to observe their customers. They must watch their customers' reactions and note their comments about the products and services provided. And, they definitely must be told to not bad-mouth a product, even if it *is* difficult to assemble. When an associate discovers anything negative from a customer, there should be a customer experience team that analyzes what can be done to remedy the situation. This is what sets apart a top business from a struggling one.

Pixel Exploration 4 - *Creepy Chicken*

Gazorkian English: "Weeed ju leek creepy ooh krid?"
American English: "Would you like crispy or grilled?"

Don't ask me to translate, "Flaark zu, zeee flarken boozdids!..." It's not very nice. Believe it or not, this Pixel, as well as all the others, is taken from a real, true-to-life case study. It may be humorous, but it is also quite sad. It is symptomatic of how the business world is flushing downward into a spiraling decline in regard to customer service. The standard for communication in the business world has been worsening for many years. But why? It is a bad problem, but it is the product of a good development, which will only increase with time.

The positive aspect is that the human race is spreading out, expanding, and races are merging globally. Due to increased transportation networks and venues, not only are people travelling more, they are intermingling and relocating to foreign nations. This is good, because it helps people to understand one another more, thus removing boundaries and prejudices. I work with people from all over the world, and the more I do, the more I grow to love them. This is a positive trend toward world peace.

The downfall to this is that until humanity eliminates the language barrier by either using technology or by creating a universal language, poor communication skills will continue to ravage and destroy ideal customer service. Many businesses lose customers, because the employees they post on the front lines to deal directly with the customers cannot communicate with them. This is frustrating to customers. It causes them to take their business elsewhere. Some may argue, "But I cannot find employees with good communication skills to work at the cash register." That may be the case, but your competitors will find a way, and they will put you out of business if you don't. Customers will gravitate toward those businesses that understand them and can be understood by them.

It is important to note that I do not refer merely to people who speak English as a second language. There are armies of employees with poor speaking skills who are born and raised on our own soil. The issue is more related to poor business management.

Often, I have seen owners from other countries travel overseas to the United States so they can live the American dream. They dream of having their own businesses, and in my industry, most of the people who want to open a franchise are from other countries. This is not bad at all, but they do not always have good communication skills themselves. Still, this is not a major issue, as long as they put a manager in charge who *does* have great communication abilities and speaks the country's native language proficiently. But they usually do not. Why? It is because managers/owners attract those like themselves, and they prefer to hire those similar to themselves. That is why, if a person from another country who barely speaks the language is hired as the manager, he will probably hire others just like him, who barely speak the language. He doesn't consider it a problem, because he communicates with them well; he doesn't know any better. He and his employees speak their native language behind the counter to each other, so the manager doesn't realize how frustrating it is to customers who cannot understand them.

There are several solutions to this dilemma. First, businesses should require verbal skills testing of all employees who deal directly with customers. If they do not pass the communication testing, they may still work for the employer, but in a different capacity; they should not interface directly with customers. There are language-skills testing services that focus on helping employers find the right employees. One is Carnegie Speech. They have an online testing service called Native Accent, which uses algorithms to analyze a person's speaking skills and scores them on a standard scale. If the person scores less than 80%, they are encouraged to take online verbal skills courses, which are able to increase speaking skills dramatically. According to their research, 80% is what is necessary to be able to communicate in the American business industry. I do not endorse any one service, but there are other services on the market that help employers. There are even some with actual technicians who conduct verbal aptitude tests over the phone. Companies with large numbers of employees, such as LightSpeed, would be wise to hire a fulltime verbal-skills tester. It would increase their profitability incredibly.

Another solution, which is often dreaded by employers, but necessary, is to pay more to the employees who work directly with customers. "That's absurd," some may challenge, but consider this. If an employer pays minimum wage to a clerk who cannot communicate with the customers, the business *will* lose customers. Make note of this: If you hire poor communicators, you *will* lose money. People tend to do business with those they can communicate with. If an employer hires a great communicator as a clerk at, say, $10/hour, he may pay a bit more, but he will increase profitability, which means he can afford to pay them more. It will add more money to his pocketbook in the long run and he will benefit from greater brand quality. Ultimately, he will be creating a better customer experience. The reality is, if an employer refuses to hire front-line employees with great customer experience skills, he is making a commitment to failure. He will put himself out of business. It is that critical of a matter.

Pixel Exploration 5 - *Smellians*

This case study is actually two related studies combined into one, and it covers a major issue in business today. Zhirbaana realized that this is a taboo issue that the business industry is afraid to broach, but it is crucial to business success, because business is universal.

We are all unique. Often, we look at another's cultures and we may criticize the very things that they criticize us about. What we don't realize is that we are all alien to one another in some way and the only way to resolve these differences is to accept them.

For example, if Zhirbaana were to move to China, she should not expect the Chinese people to change and accept her. She should change to fit their culture, even becoming the epitome of Chinese culture and living; in doing so, she would honor them. This would grant her the approval to be accepted into their community. In business, it is a rite of passage. A person who moves to another country should embrace that country's way of life and traditions completely. That does not mean that they should not share their own culture with those interested in broadening their understanding of the world. Regardless, even if they have different ideals, they must submit to that culture first in order to maintain the peace and to survive. This is how I believe the business world will be the final catalyst to world peace.

People must strive to become more educated in the ways of human cultures, protocols, and etiquette, especially if they relocate to another country. America is one of the most open and accepting countries in the world;

it is known as the "melting pot," but even immigrants need to understand that American business has a certain air to it. It is an important facet that may not be overlooked. To do so is to commit business suicide.

The second person Zhirbaana had consulted with in the case study was an amazing person, but he was so deep-rooted in his own former country's culture that he made most Americans feel uncomfortable. He did not even realize it. After their frank meeting, he came to a complete realization that he needed to make some changes if he was going to do business within his very rural American community. Zhirbaana had him read the book, <u>American Ways</u>, by Gary Althen, and she explained to him common American hygiene and etiquette. It was like opening a new world to him. Contrary to what most critics might say, he was not offended at all. Of course, it may just be his personality or his drive to succeed, but he accepted her advice and evolved to fit his new culture. Today, he is a great businessman and I applaud him for his accomplishments. I consider him a role-model for others who move to America wishing to become entrepreneurs.

The primary point to learn from this Pixel is that in order to do business in any community, one must become like that community, even becoming like a celebrity to that community. How does one do that? It is simple. All one must do to be accepted into any community, is to become like the elected officials within that community. Why? It is because people elect those whom they like and with whom they feel most comfortable. Elected officials exemplify the people of their community in not only ideals and philosophies, but also in image and lifestyle. The only way an official may become elected is to be accepted by a majority of the voters. If the majority of the voters, i.e. the financial decision makers, in that community approve of a prime official, if you model them, they will likely approve of you as well. If you want to do business in a community, regardless of where you are from, I encourage you to get to know the elected officials and learn from them. Take them out to dinner. Support them and they will teach you a deeper understanding of what it takes to have your business accepted within your community.

Pixel Exploration 6 - *Rinosceron Angst*

This case study reveals important lessons. First, it shows us how often employees reflect their managers. It is interesting to see how much employees try to emulate their leadership. Psychologically, they look up to their supervisors as their role-models. They unconsciously think that, "Well, my boss got where he is by being the way he is, so that is exactly how I need to be." What top management may not realize is that a minor eccentricity or character flaw in an employee, though it may be well masked, can become quite a behemoth to deal with if that employee is promoted.

Consider Bort. Before he became manager, he was a very proud, matter-of-fact, in-your-face type of employee, but he was smart. He took great care to not show that side of himself to his superiors. Bort's colleagues saw it all too well, and they were threatened by him. That is why he was rarely challenged. His manager saw this as a good thing, causing him to perceive Bort as a bold leader who was not afraid to get the job done. In reality, Bort was a bully who did get what he wanted because people were too afraid to cross him. Some may say this is a good trait for leadership, but it is not a good trait for customer service. One may be able to fool a supervisor for a while, but he cannot fool customers. Customers can sense when someone truly cares for them; Bort did not. He didn't take flak from customers, and unfortunately, he trained his team to be the same way, thus causing a black hole of deplorable customer service. Not only did he damage his company's name brand, he nearly caused their entire team to be laid off and they did not even know it. Sadly, since the company had endorsed Bort as a manager, the employees idealized and magnified his attitude and customer philosophy. Even though he was no longer with the company, his spirit lived on, especially in Lih.

The next lesson we can learn from this case study is from Qirk. He did two important things that turned their business in the right direction. He changed their customer philosophy into that of true customer service. He showed his new team how critical it was to serve their customers in an excellent manner. He put flesh on his philosophy by relating how having happy customers meant receiving what they desired, whether it be a new hovercraft or a dream vacation. Qirk made them realize that every positive customer experience led them one step closer to reaching their own personal fulfillment.

The second thing we can learn from Qirk is that he conveyed to his employees that their own success was his goal. He was the epitome of quality customer service and he modeled superior customer service to his team by treating them the way he wanted them to treat their customers. He wanted his team to be successful, regardless of whether they worked for the company or not.

Qirk was put into a tough situation where he had to consider terminating Lih. Instead of giving an ultimatum to, "shape up or ship out," he let her know that he wanted her to be successful, whether she stayed in their company or not. He put the choice into her hands. He gave her the power to decide her own fate, all the while letting her know that he had her best interests at heart. By doing this, he again exemplified model customer service, just like he might tell a disgruntled customer, "I am sorry that you are not satisfied with our service (or product), but my goal is for you to be happy. If we cannot help you, will you let me help you find another company that can?"

Qirk's positive actions helped Lih to realize that she was fortunate to be working with someone who had her best interest at heart; she realized that he would help her. She experienced a realization through their meeting, recognizing that what Bort taught her was detrimental and had been hurting her chances of success. Fortunately, she did change and grew into an ideal employee, herself evolving into the epitome of model customer service.

Finally, we learn from this case study that business success is only achieved by having a superior customer service philosophy. We see that failure in management to convey ideal customer experiences leads to potential bankruptcy. On the other hand, success in providing great customer satisfaction equates to financial business success.

Pixel Exploration 7 - *Scorian Squietches*

In this case study, squietches represent general standards of cleanliness. It should be common business sense, really, especially in an increasingly germophobic era, but it is surprising how many businesses do not think such things matter. The truth is, they do.

For those who wonder how cleanliness could be a matter of customer service, it is important to understand what customer service is. Customer service is *the manner in which one serves a customer*. Consider that one word, "manner." It is the *way* customers are treated. The manner relates to their entire experience involving a brand. This could start from the point they see a business's sign at an intersection, but it goes deeper than that. It could be the point that, while sitting at that intersection, they see trash strewn across the parking lot, or paint peeling off the sides of the building. *What customers see of the care you invest into your business, is how they perceive you will take care of them.*

Many customers, like me, are extremely picky about cleanliness. If I walk up to a restaurant with smudgy handprints on the windows, and the door handle looks dirty, I will turn around and leave. I am not alone; many customers react this way. But why? It is because when we see how unclean a business is on the outside, where people are looking, how much more filthy is it in the kitchen, behind closed doors, where no one can see? We imagine that there are cockroaches skittering across the plates; we picture rats crawling through the food. The imagination runs wild, and squietches seem like a real possibility.

In one independent study conducted by a local nonprofit organization, it was discovered that the number one thing that their prospects looked for before deciding to join an organization was how clean the restrooms were. Think about that. I have no doubt that restroom cleanliness is also a prime factor for these prospects when they decide which restaurant to eat at, or which convenience store to stop at. Today's customers are cautious, and rather picky, but they can afford to be. Their choices for doing business are many, so if they see a building sign with burned out lights, or nests in the channel letters, they think, "How unprofessional." If they enter an office and see trash on the floors, or dirty, stained carpets, they think, "Yuck, this is the last time I come here."

As I mentioned, success is in the details. Customers must see everything as being perfectly ideal. Otherwise, they will unconsciously perceive that there is something wrong with your business, and when the chance comes to take their business to a newer, better, and cleaner alternative, they will.

Businesses must not fool themselves into thinking that there really is such a thing as customer loyalty. It is a fallacy. Customers have no obligation to be loyal to any business. Why should they? They do not sign a marriage certificate to commit till "death do you part." They reside in a capitalistic world and their choices of which businesses to patronize are virtually endless. Therefore, it is every business's responsibility to create and maintain high standards. It is critical to remember that every aspect of a customer's experience must be considered a standard part of customer service. It is this standard that customers expect and deserve.

PASSION FORMULA

Pixel Exploration 8 – *Zed & Ot*

This is a fascinating case study, because Zed and Ot are both correct to a degree. Ot shared that he saw business as a numbers game; he thought that getting more customers in and out quickly meant more sales for him. In my experience, that is somewhat true. The more customers one assists, the more sales he will typically make.

Zed stated, "I keep my customers, because they like the service I provide and they know they can trust me. It's all about those two things: service and trust." This is true also. So, which employee is (A) a better revenue generator, and which is (B) better for the business? The two are not always synonymous.

Consider this extreme scenario. Ot blasts through one-hundred customers in one week; he sells to twenty-five, but offends the majority of his customers. His sales numbers are high, compared to Zed's. Zed is only able to have thirty quality, in-depth presentations, but makes sales to twenty customers. He does not sell to ten, though he does not offend any of them. Ot makes more money than Zed, though Ot's closing rate is 25%, while Zed's is 66%. What this reveals is that Zed is a better closer when he does make a presentation, but Ot generates more immediate revenue for the company than Zed. So, in such cases, employees like Ot are more likely to be promoted, because they produce greater short-term results.

The reality is, Ot is burning through the company's market, destroying everything in his path. Sure, he may sell to 25 customers, but most leave with a bad customer experience, and they tell others about it. This detrimentally impacts the company's business in the long term.

Zed, on the other hand, makes virtually everyone he meets happy, even those who opt to take their business elsewhere due to better pricing at a competitor. He sells less, but he increases positive brand awareness for the company, thus ensuring slow but steady business growth.

Consider this, if the business owner likes Ot's style of doing business, and he fires Zed due to low sales, but hires more associates like Ot, their profitability may increase greatly. The atmosphere will change to that of a shark feeding frenzy and the customers in the market will be gobbled up quickly. The owner may think he is a genius, but the day will come when the dam will burst. The market will not put up with such poor customer experiences for long. It is critical to remember that businesses cannot fool the market. People are not ignorant. They know whether or not a business truly has their best interests at heart. Customers are savvy, and it doesn't take long for them to figure out that they are being used and taken advantage of. Businesses that take the Ot approach eventually become bankrupt. I've seen it happen.

Contrarily, what would happen if the business owner let Ot go, but hired a team of associates just like Zed? The business would grow slowly, but it would be sure growth, which would strengthen the brand. The market would hear about the excellent customer experiences and the business would be poised for great success, but it would not happen overnight.

This is where young businesses often fail. They don't always recognize that strong businesses usually grow slowly. There are no shortcuts to quality customer service. Inexperienced businesses often shoot out of the starting gate desiring quick growth, and they sometimes do whatever it takes to get it. This can cause many mistakes in customer service. The only way to avoid these mistakes is to establish a monumental philosophy within the business that states, *every individual customer experience matters. It is not a matter of quantity, but of the quality of our service that will determine our success.*

There is a surefire way for a business owner to determine if an employee is an Ot or a Zed. All he has to do is follow Zed's example of asking for customer feedback, as is exemplified in Feature D. If he discovers he has an Ot, that does not mean he should terminate him. It is possible that Ot may have the skill set necessary for success, but he may not have the right customer philosophy or attitude needed. Ot might be a great employee if he learned Zed's approach to customer service, and he may be able to gain more quality customer experiences than even Zed, if trained properly. It is a matter of proper customer experience training and mentoring by management, but the key to perfect customer service does go beyond simply training and mentoring.

If Ot and Zed are given the same number of customers to work with, it would be obvious to all that Zed is the superior customer service representative. In this Pixel, what can be gleaned is that Zed exudes sheer passion and he has the right philosophy.

When I was a young man, I thought business philosophies were like fluffy clouds; they looked big and lofty, but I considered them to be without much substance and useless. I wanted to know the tangible tricks of the trade and focused solely on pragmatic methods for success. As I matured in my business experience, I realized that the processes, methods, and tangible tools mean absolutely nothing without the right mental philosophy. One can use a proven checklist, or process, and achieve base results, but he will probably never realize optimum results.

Consider our case study. If the owner had promoted Zed and told him to retrain Ot, Zed could show Ot all the techniques he uses and he could even write an entire script for Ot to follow when talking to customers. But until Ot completely changes his internal business philosophy, he will never experience the same type of success that Zed does with customers. Ot must come to a realization that his personal view of business and customers is tainted. Customers are not "numbers," in a game that is to be won so that he can earn a fat paycheck.

Zed gives us glimpses into his philosophy when he says such things as, "I try to look at things from my customer's point of view. I treat them as I would my own family … they need someone to empathize with them; that's what I do … they like the service I provide and they know they can trust me. It's all about those two things: service and trust … the more quality time I invest in creating a great experience for my customers, the more my customers are willing to invest in me … My customers are the best, and I really do love them; I mean it."

Zed shows his passion by his obvious love for his job and for his customers. It is this attitude and customer philosophy that makes him superior. Zed is also likely to be a better employee and associate to work with. Honestly, who would you rather work with, Zed or Ot? Zed's exuberance is contagious and stimulating. It makes people feel happy. His philosophy must be replicated in Ot. Only then can Ot be trained and mentored in the other practical methods of customer service. Changing one's internal philosophy, however, is the greatest challenge of all.

So how does one go about changing his business philosophy? He has to be constantly exposed to the proper philosophies and the thinking behind them. For example, if Zed and Ot were to have a meeting with their employer, he might ask them questions like, "Who are our customers to you?" "How do you feel about them?" "How do you think you make our customers feel through your service?" "What do you think our purpose as a business is?" This question really gets to the heart of the matter. Ot might respond, "To make money." Zed might say, "To help people experience new and exciting things in life through travel."

The key to philosophy adjustment is to ask a lot of questions and to validate the right responses. For example, Zed's response to their purpose as a business could be followed up on by his manager with a statement or email letter affirming, "We are here solely to help as many customers as possible to experience great new things in life through travel. We have to remember that. We are sharing something greater with them that will change their lives. We don't do this for the money. We do it to impact people and to enrich them. This is what makes our job so exciting." It is critical that this type of philosophy be endorsed, because the reality is, people are not really motivated to work for money. If money is the primary motivating factor for employees, their enthusiasm will wane, because they will eventually come to the realization, "Is this what my entire life really amounts to? A paycheck? There's got to be more to life."

Employees must sense that there is something greater that they can experience and achieve through your business. It must give them a feeling of achievement and purpose. That is what the correct business philosophy is for. Once employees share the proper philosophy, their sense of wonderment and passion will spread to your customers and that is when true growth occurs. This is what Zed exemplifies. Once an employee grasps the right business philosophy, he will not only be a powerhouse of productivity, he will experience great upward growth and mobility in the company. He will achieve his own personal goals in life and yours as well. This is what makes the passion formula work, and it is why having a solid philosophy is so important.

Pixel Exploration 9 – *Bliss on Averocia*

I often talk to aspiring entrepreneurs who want help in starting up a new business. Many of them have the same preconceived notions. They rattle off clichés like, "Location, location, location," because they believe that the location will be the prime factor that will contribute to their success. They want to see demographics and compare markets to determine which one is the best, in terms of income, population, etc. Others believe marketing is the main factor. They think if they dump enough money into advertising, customers will flock to their doors.

These factors are important to consider, because success does lie in the minute details, but in my experience, the one thing that makes a business successful is not so much the location or the marketing, as it is the person operating it. I don't mean that the operator has to have an MBA; I have seen highly educated people fail in business. I have also seen people with absolutely no business experience succeed, simply because of their attitude, people skills, and communication abilities.

Face it, what is business? It is simply one person offering something that another person wants, and they agree to an exchange for it. It is not a complex operation, though we make it out to be. The very first business transaction that happened between cavemen probably went like this:

- *1st Business Man:* "Ugh, Thag have rock!"

147

- *1st Customer:* "Ooh, rock! Bork want rock! Me give stick for rock?"
- *1st Business Man:* "Ugh, stick good. You take rock. Come again soon!"

Why would one want to exchange something with another? It is because we have a need or want. If we need something and only one other person has it, the value of that thing is high. There are some businesses that have a virtual monopoly on a product or service and the value of what they offer is high. Consumers are willing to pay anything to acquire it. Thus, the business knows that their customers are desperate for what they have, so they sometimes abuse that privilege. This means their customer service skills are almost certainly lacking.

On the other hand, if there are many providers of a product or service, the customer has many vendors to choose from. With the quality of the product/service and the price being fairly equal, the customer will likely choose to do business simply because he likes one person better than another. In the caveman scenario, the situation might eventually become like this:

- *1st Business Man:* "Ugh, Thag have rock!"
- *2nd Business Man:* "Oh! Dort have rock, too! Better rock! Me like Bork! Bork want rock?"
- *1st Customer:* "Ooh, Thag rock … Dort rock! Hmm, Bork want Dort rock. Me like Dort! Me give Dort stick for rock?"
- *2nd Business Man:* "Ugh, Stick good. Bork good! You take rock. Come again soon!"

- *1st Business Man:* "Ah, zug! Thag mad!"

This is the reality that we live in today. Customers realize that they have many options and the truth of the matter is, most will buy from a business simply because they like the manager, clerk, or the owner better. The commodities of the future are intangible things like people skills, communication skills, passion, and a positive attitude.

Consider this scenario. Two parents are looking for a tutor for their five-year-old child. They visit several different ones and listen to various presentations on what each has to offer, as well as the different pricing structures. The parents are overwhelmed by it all; the dad turns to his wife and says, "Who do you think we should use?" She responds, "They all sound good in different ways, but I'm not sure. There is so much information on all of them … I don't know …" The mother turns to her little girl and asks, "What do you think? Which tutor do you want to go to?" The little girl smiles, twirling back and forth, and replies, "I like the last one! She was nice to me; she gave me a lollipop!" The dad says, "Well, that settles it! That's your new tutor!"

It may seem silly, but consumers often make purchasing decisions based on feelings, and gut-instincts. They are overwhelmed by the options set before them and they don't know which is the better product or service, so who do they go with? They tend to choose the business which is represented by great staff who make them *feel* good. If they like an associate, because he is outgoing, friendly, and energized, they will do business with him.

This is why, in our Pixel, the Holophonix Corporation grew when Bliss took over operations.

Bliss exemplifies the ideal business person. I have no doubt that she is the type of person who could make virtually any business successful, not because of her great business acumen or training, but simply because people are attracted to her; they trust her, and want to do business with her.

To be successful, businesses must acquire employees like Bliss to be the *face* of their operations, or they must train their associates to be able to have the same type of skills that Bliss embodies. This means that for perfect customer service training, front-line employees (i.e., those who interact directly with customers) must be trained in three primary areas: (1) People skills, (2) Communication skills, and (3) Passion for the business. These are challenging skills to train, because they are intangible. But, they are a must.

Some candidates for improvement in these areas may look like rough stones, but underneath are truly gems, simply in need of polishing. They need the jagged edges knocked off and to be constantly polished until they shine. One must be able to take that person and create them as a sort of celebrity within their own community. They have to understand that they represent the brand in and out of the business.

On occasion, I see that a company may have just the right people with just the right skills, but they are working in the wrong capacity. For example, a firm has a fiery, inspirational go-getter working in the back office. She is motivated and loves to talk to people. Everyone in the office loves her, but she never deals with customers. She spends her time working on spreadsheets. She is good at it, but the business might profit more if she was working in the front interacting directly with customers. Instead, the company has a depressed young woman working at the front; she gets annoyed with people easily and she is not inspired at all. She is a hard worker, but the staff knows not to cross her in the mornings, especially if she hasn't had her coffee yet. If these two employees were to switch roles, they might be happier and more productive, but most of all, the customers would be happier and general customer service would improve. Overall, because the customer experience would improve, profits would increase.

Some people cannot learn people skills, because it is not a matter of their ability but of them having the right mindset. For those willing to learn, with aptitude, people skills can be trained through role-play and modeling. The trainer models how to respond to customers first, and the employee role-plays the response, practicing with many different scenarios. The employee also needs to practice socializing with others in group settings. They need to get involved in social activities and networks. The more people they interact with, the better their skills will become.

Communication skills can be acquired and improved upon by having the trainee practice speaking, preferably in front of groups. Employees can enroll in speech classes or join a Rotary Club. Some may even need to take diction courses, which are available online. Role-play is also important for improving communication skills, if one is open to constructive criticism. The trainer must provide honest feedback and the trainee must be malleable, and able to change.

Passion, probably the most important virtue of all, can be trained by modeling it. One must also establish a positive work atmosphere that is conducive to generating positive feelings and inspiration. Passion begins with leadership. It is a fire that grows and spreads virally from one associate to another. Businesses must develop Passion coordinators who focus on increasing team spirit and morale, just as a pep squad would work to excite the home team. The managers are the cheerleaders who provoke the crowd into a frenzy of unquenchable corporate patriotism and synergy. Those who exude the greatest passion and fervor must be rewarded and exalted in the ranks, because they exemplify the true spirit and ideals that others are to follow. This is how passion is conceived and grown within great businesses.

Pixel Exploration 10 – *Y-Knots*

As Ixsa realized, we are in the people business. Or let me rephrase that – we are in the, "make people happy," business. In this Pixel, we see Ixsa change from being a self-centered, failing businessman to becoming a giving, people-centric success. Customer service is all about making people happy. If a business makes a customer happy, the customer will likely do business with them, or may refer others to do so. Every employee, manager, and business owner should have a 'Y-Knot," on their desk or hanging on their wall. They serve to remind us of why we are here.

In dealing with customers, we must be keenly aware of their needs, in effort to seek out "Y-Knot," moments. For example, a customer walks into a large store and asks a clerk where a specific product is. Often, an average clerk will say, "I think that is in aisle nine," or he might even say, "I'm not sure," simply brushing the customer off, as if he was a nuisance. The better clerk would say, "I'm glad you asked. Let me show you," and he takes him directly to the product; he thinks to himself, "Why not?" If the clerk does not know where the item is, he might say, "You know, I'm not sure where that is either, but we will find it together," again thinking, "Why not?" He doesn't rest until the customer has found exactly what he is looking for. The average clerk asks himself, "Why should I help? Why should I care?" The better clerk may ask the same questions, but he answers, "Why not?" Seriously, what is it going to hurt? Going above and beyond the call of duty only helps one to become better; becoming better is what escalates one person over another. These are the details that generate success.

In this Pixel, Ixsa mentions, "I have even taken it one step further. When I sense that a customer has a need or desire, I challenge myself to say, 'Why not help him?' or 'Why not surprise him with something?'" This is a critical detail of success, which I call *engagement*. Engagement is the act of taking customer service to the next level, in much the same way a dating couple takes their relationship to the next level by becoming engaged in marriage. I define customer engagement as thinking and acting beyond normal expectations; it is courting the customer. Just like a man may court a woman by sending her several dozen roses, or by lavishing her with expensive gifts, a keen business person courts customers by giving them more than they expect; they thrill them with surprise.

Nowadays, most businesses provide only the bare basics in product quality and service standards. In Pixel 8, we see Zed exemplifying the qualities of engagement. Zed starts out offering his customer something to drink. He gives him a tour of his office. He shares with the customer about their history. He gives above and beyond. Zed relates with the customer, courting him, step by step, until the customer is completely engaged in the business.

The early steps of engagement, much like dating, are akin to expressing to the customer, "I want to get to know you. I want to get to know everything about you. I want us to build a long and lasting relationship with one another. Tell me all about you."

On a first date, the man attempts to look and act his best in order to impress the woman. Likewise, in a first-time customer experience, the business person must look and act his best in effort to impress the customer. On that first date, the man, smitten by her lovely beauty, wit, and charm, wants to know everything about the woman; he urges her to tell him everything about her. Similarly, the sharp business person persuades the customer to open up and share with him, so they may deepen their bond.

Through such sharing, the business person learns some, "Why not?" moments. He may learn that the customer loves the Denver Broncos; he may discover that his favorite food is Mexican food; he may find that the customer absolutely loves pecans. The business person thinks, "Why not do something special with that knowledge?" He emails the customer an article about the Broncos, which thrills him. The customer is shocked that he remembered. The next time he comes in, the business person gives him a homemade pecan praline; again, the customer is pleasantly surprised. Such acts are simple, but they make powerful statements to the customer; they say to him, "I know you and I care about you." They make him think, "If he treats me this well when we are not conducting business, I cannot imagine how well he will treat me when we do." It also makes the customer want to do extensive business with him and to help him find other new customers. It creates loyal, dedicated customers, who grow to love and support the business. This is the power of engagement.

Feature A

Identifying Customer Levels

How do we achieve a great customer experience? Modeling in action – Example:

A. President – The President must look at his VP's/managers as his own personal customers, striving to support and coach them with passion and vigor.

B. VP's/Managers – They, too, look at their staff as their customers, not employees. Management works to provide optimal support, follow-up, inspiration, and passion to their staff/customers. This causes them to have a great experience.

C. Staff – Following the example of their leaders, they treat their customers with great care, striving to impassion and inspire them, so they model the same behavior to their own customers. Employee turnover decreases.

D. Customers – They are excited and invigorated by their experience, because they receive the highest support and care from staff. They reflect that same enthusiasm to their friends and community, causing the business to grow. It causes them to be happy, motivated, and passionate. Such a customer is productive on behalf of the business and will produce great growth for the company.

Feature B

Customer Experience Program Checklist

To be used by corporate management for their associates. This also may be used by franchisors for franchisees:

❑ Provide the **"Management Feedback Request Template,"** (Feature C) to associates.
   o **Evaluate the results** – Consult with each associate as needed.

❑ Develop a **Customer Experience Training** utilizing the principles outlined in this book.

❑ **Communicate with all associates individually** – One month prior to the Customer Experience Training, use the following script as a guideline:
   o *"As you may know, our company is implementing a new and exciting customer experience program that is going to escalate our customer service to a whole new level. We have a special guest speaker who will be presenting on it at the next meeting on (give date), and I want you to attend. Can you commit to coming to that meeting?"*

❑ **Associate attends the training.** If an associate cannot attend, email him the presentation via DVD or webinar link and ask him to watch it by a certain date.

❑ **Immediately after the meeting, schedule a conference** (by phone or in-person) with each associate. Be passionate, positive, and confident. Give your associates the tools for the program:

- o Provide them the **"Customer Feedback Request,"** template (Feature D).
- o Provide them the **"Positive Customer Meeting Checklist."** (Feature E)

❑ **Meet with your associates in person** – Review the forms above with associates. Read each bullet point aloud on the form and ensure that they understand it and can implement the process. Role-play the "**Positive Customer Meeting Checklist**" (Feature E) with them, physically walking them through the entire process.

❑ **Schedule a deadline** by which they will give the "**Customer Feedback Request**" (Feature D) to all their customers.

❑ **Follow-Up** – One week after the Customer Feedback Request (Feature D) is sent out, ask associates what feedback they received from the feedback requests. Be positive and do not criticize their efforts or results.

- o Associates conduct the **"Positive Support Check – Customer."** (Feature F) with all customers.

- o   Associates submit the completed forms to management.

❑ **Monthly** – Managers contact associates and conduct the **"Positive Support Check - Associates."** (Feature G)

- o   Submit the completed form to upper management.

❑ **Biannually** – Prior to mid-year and year-end evaluations, management emails associates the **"Management Feedback Request Template,"** (Feature C)

- o   **Evaluate the results** – Consult with each associate and manager as needed.

- o   **Include feedback results** – Add comments to each evaluation.

❑ **Annually** – Attend at least one customer service/motivational training and invite your associates to join you. It will build better employee/customer relationships and experiences.

❑ **Follow-up** – Regularly, utilize tools, videos, training modules, books, and materials with your associates to keep them motivated and inspired.

Feature C

Management Feedback Request Template

Each manager is to customize this template and provide it to each of their employees:

"As your supervisor, it is my goal to ensure that you receive the right guidance, training, and support so that you may be able to accomplish your job to the best of your ability, while achieving the success you desire. I have been striving to make sure that my quality of managerial service to the company has been top quality and I was wondering if you felt I served you well as your manager. Would you please email or write me your feedback as to how I have performed in this capacity? I would appreciate it, as it will help me to improve in my own abilities and service; it will also further our company's goals. Please email your feedback to me. Or if you would like to comment directly to my supervisor, you may email (Supervisor's name) at SupervisorsEmailAddress@CompanyDomain.com and let him/her know what you thought. Your comments will be kept in confidence. I greatly appreciate it."

PASSION FORMULA

Feature D

Customer Feedback Request Template

Each associate is to customize this template and provide it to each of their customers:

"I have been working to make sure that my quality of service to our customers has been as great as it can be, and I was wondering if you felt I served you well and efficiently. If so, would you mind emailing me your feedback as to how I performed? I would appreciate it, as it will help me to improve my service to others. Please email your feedback to me. Or if you would like to comment on my performance directly to my supervisor, please email (Supervisor's name) at SupervisorsEmailAddress@CompanyDomain.com and let him/her know what you thought. Your responses will be kept confidential. I greatly appreciate it."

PASSION FORMULA

Feature E

Positive Customer Meeting Checklist

To be used by associates in advance to prepare for each initial customer meeting, when applicable:

Initial Calls

- ❑ **Immediate Response** – Return all and any emails and calls within 30 minutes or less, if possible.
- ❑ **Be passionate, positive, and confident on the phone** – Schedule a meeting, when applicable.

Pre-Meeting Preparation

- ❑ **Signage working and lit up.**
- ❑ **Storefront/Facade presentable** – No trash on the sidewalk or parking lot; doors and glass is clean.
- ❑ **Store/Office interior** – Clean, and presentable. Entrance and restrooms clean, trashcans empty.
- ❑ **All front doors unlocked.**
- ❑ **All lights on.**
- ❑ **Coffee, tea, and/or water ready and available.** Candy (optional) available for children.
- ❑ **MINDSET CHECK –** Place yourself in the proper frame of mind prior to the meeting. Generate positive thoughts, and feelings. Motivate yourself internally, so that you exude passion.

❑ **SMILE - Greet customers at the door personally and heartily** – open the door for them. Always be prepared in advance for their arrival. With excitement, say:
  o *"Welcome!"*
  o *"Did you find us okay?"*

❑ **Introductions** - Any present staff must pause and greet the guests as soon as they arrive. If there are any additional guests, children, etc. with them, ask them their names. Offer guests a drink.

❑ **Tour** – Show them the facilities, talk about the company's history, and provide your credentials. Choose one element (image/picture) that you can tell a story about that is exciting or will pique their interest.

❑ **Build a relationship -** Sit down with customers and say, *"I would like to get to know you. Please, tell me about yourself."* Find one thing that the customer is interested in as they talk – it should be the spark that connects you to the customer. **Example** – The customer states, *"My daughter loves soccer. She just won a medal!"* You may find common interests and could respond, *"What a coincidence! My daughter loves it too! What team is she on? I would love to see her play…"* Make a connection.

❑ **After a connection has been made, say:** *"What can I do to assist you today?"*

- ❑ **Make notes** – Keep handwritten notes about family names, likes, dislikes, habits, problems, etc.
- ❑ **Begin official service/product presentation.**
- ❑ **Look for any *"Y-Knot?"* moments in the meeting.** **Example** – *"You mentioned you liked stamp collecting. I just so happen to have some unique stamps from Paraguay that I would like to give you. Would you like to have them?" (Why not?)*
- ❑ **Follow-up** – Schedule your customer's next meeting, if applicable.
- ❑ Note the next experience contact point, call, or meeting:

_____

Follow-up Plan/Notes:

_____

_____

_____

_____

_____

_____

_____

PASSION FORMULA

Feature F

Positive Support Check - Customer

To be used by associates with their customers on a monthly basis and submitted to management:

Customer Printed Name: _____
Meeting Date: _____

"How are you?" Notes: _____
"How is your family?" Notes: _____
"Is there anything I can do to further serve you?" Notes:
_____
"Do you feel that you or someone you know could further benefit from our products/services?" Notes: _____
Were there any *"Y-Knot?"* moments in this meeting?
Notes: _____
Next experience contact point, call, or meeting: _____
Follow-up Plan/Notes: _____

Associate Printed Name: _____
Signature: _____

PASSION FORMULA

Feature G

Positive Support Check - Associates

To be used by management for their respective employees on a monthly basis and submitted to their supervisors.

Associate Printed Name: _____

Meeting Date: _____

"How are you?" Notes: _____

"How is your family?" Notes: _____

"What can I do to support you?" Notes: _____

"Do you feel that you need any additional training or guidance?" Notes: _____

Were there any *"Y-Knot?"* moments in this meeting? Notes: _____

Next experience contact point, call, or meeting: _____

Follow-up Plan/Notes:

_____

Manager Printed Name: _____

Signature: _____

PASSION FORMULA

Feature H

Compendium of Elements

Element 1 (E1): Embrace your employer. Love her deeply.

Element 2 (E2): Corporate change. It is injected into a corporate body, usually by a new executive leader. This element is unstable in nature. It may be accepted by the corporate body at first, but after the reaction occurs, it may slowly undergo a process of violent rejection. If not controlled by other stable elements (such as element Be1, etc.), its powerful oxidization nature will cause the executive(s) to be eliminated, quite possibly destroying the whole of the corporate body.

Element 3 (E3): Reprogram your mind. Withdraw. Refocus. Your purpose must be to change your daily pattern, or routine, and realign your mental status quo to become healthier. This may mean that you need to spend a week with an inspirational guru you admire, or that you should attend a motivational boot camp or inspirational event. Regardless, you must determine that whatever activity you choose to undertake, it must reboot your cognitive faculty well enough that you do not return with the same mental state as when you left. This must be accomplished on a regular basis.

Element 4 (E4): Cling to a passionate mentor. Your mentor does not necessarily need to be someone in your field of work or study. He or she does, however, have to be someone inspirational, who will cause you to catch the fires of passion so

that you can continue to burn with motivation and fervency
after you depart.

Element 5 (E5): *Create. Allow yourself to be innovative and
creative in your role. Approach your supervisor and suggest
new ideas that will increase productivity or will inspire your
associates. Innovation will fuel your passion and will generate
more excitement about what you do.*

Element 6 (E6): *Personal ownership. Empowerment. Whether
the employee has tangible shares in the company or not, he/she
must be granted personal ownership of it. The employer must
instill the sense of personal ownership within every associate.
This element generates allegiance and strong feelings of
commitment toward the employer. Every associate must become
a devotee. This empowerment is the catalyst to creating great
customer service.*

Element 7 (E7): *Customer engagement. Inspire and engage the
customer. Use this "element of surprise" by giving them service
beyond their expectations. Consider what the customer would
expect from the typical transaction and give them more, to the
point where they say, "Wow!" That is the proper amount of this
element that must be added to the successful customer experience
equation.*

Element 8 (E8): *Model the experience. The employer must
model the sensation of corporate passion to its employees with
intensity. It is the employer's responsibility to inspire, excite,
and motivate associates. Employees must strive to stir up the*

power of passion within themselves. They, too, must exemplify this experience to their customers.

Element 9 (E9): *Court your customer. Make him/her a part of your family. Instill personal feelings of trust, so that your customer grows 100% loyal to you. Court each new customer, as you would court a new potential spouse. Give them your full commitment and expect theirs in return. Engage them and experience a wonderful business marriage, for life.*

Element 10 (E10): *Identify all customer levels (Feature A). There is never just one level of customer who exists externally outside of the company. Employees are also "internal" customers who exist at various levels within the company. There are no "superiors" in a business. Determine who your true customer is for every level of management, starting with the President, as the president's internal customers are the VP's and upper management. Customer service must transition from a bland, two-dimensional, horizontal-ideology to a vertical, three-dimensional level, penetrating every department, impacting all employees and associates at every level. Only then will proper customer service reach out and impact the external customer.*

Element 11 (E11): *Customer feedback. (Refer to Features C and D) Every level of customer must provide feedback and every associate must be evaluated by their direct customers, even all the way up to the President. This feedback is a primary factor in annual and mid-year evaluations. It is used to determine annual raises and bonuses.*

Element 12 (E12): *Personal accountability. Do not expect others to do what you know needs to be done. Take it upon yourself and model it for them. Show them your exuberance and passion for your work. Decide to be the one who exudes greatness in your work. Become the epitome of greatness, because greatness competes with no one.*

Element 13 (E13): *Be the spark. Intensify your energy and passion within your company. Ignite all those you come into contact with. Excite and inspire. Let them feel your energy, even as you enter the room. Consider all those around you as inert elements that are waiting for an intense flame to ignite them. Be that flame. With patience, intensity, and confidence, you will cause your company to catch the fire of passion. Together, with your associates, as one corporate entity, you will amplify your powers; you will burn greater, brighter, and more powerful than thermite.*

Element 14 (E14): *Create positive experiences with your customers. The only negative experiences should be accidental, and scarce at that. If you have enough positive "experience deposits" with your customers, they will overlook any accidental negative "experience withdrawals." This is how you build an overall positive customer-experience relationship.*

Element 15 (E15): *Be content. Be happy and successful in the role you are in. You may not be the CEO of your company, but determine the good aspects of your position and set your mind at being the best at your job that you can be. Eliminate all negative thoughts; strive to be positive and uplifting to the associates around you. Life is short and every minute of it is precious, so* *don't waste one second of it moaning or yearning for what isn't or may never be.*

PASSION FORMULA

Index

PASSION FORMULA

PASSION FORMULA

PASSION FORMULA

The New Customer Experience

Marty D. Fish, CFE

Enjoy these other fine books by Great Hope Publishing:

Trokosi, by Marty D. Fish. *The inspirational story of an African teenager who was taken to be a sex slave of the gods, called the Trokosi, in a Voodoo temple. The story, from her personal diary, tells how she was horribly tortured and almost died. It conveys her daring escape and how she came to a realization of the truth about the Voodoo gods, the temple priests, and about the power of belief itself.*

Snerfy Cat Meets Prancy Finch, by Mister Fish. *"Flick! Flick! Flick!" goes Snerfy Cat's tail, as he seeks a little birdie to fill his tummy so it "does not go Ba-Rump anymore." As fate has it, on this lucky day he finds just such a morsel, a sweet little finch named Prancy. In this fun and surprising little tale, Prancy gives Snerfy much more than he could have ever expected. Prancy does not fill Snerfy's tummy, "but his whole heart instead!" This is a bright, lovely, and positive picture story book, which all children will love and adore. It truly is a modern day classic among the world of hardback children's literature.*

The Transformation of Six, by Dr. J.D. Thorogood.
Experience the exciting, true life story of the artist known as Six, who shares his personal Sentrionic Transformation and adventures with the Centrix himself, Xion Armani.

The Book of The Centrix: Xion Armani, by Xion Armani. *If it is a true story, as it claims to be, The Book of the Centrix is no doubt the greatest book ever written. The author is a man living between two worlds. "This writing is nothing other than my real encounter with a supra-human (alien) presence… I know this is all so hard to believe, but please hear my story. I hope you will take a moment so that I may share with you what I have seen, felt, and experienced. This book is my unbelievable experience into reality, a surreal reality."*

GREAT HOPE PUBLISHING™

Book cover artwork design by Gloria Fish.

Published in the United States of America

Paperback Standard Version
ISBN-10: 0985913762
ISBN-13: 978-0-9859137-6-2

www.ingramcontent.com/pod-product-compliance
Lightning Source LLC
Chambersburg PA
CBHW071550200326
41519CB00021BB/6682